Praise for *Chi Kung in*

T0266447

"Greg's dynamic presentation of Chi Kung has become an integral aspect of our recovery model at Central Recovery Treatment in Las Vegas. I am very excited to have the material available in such a user friendly format as his book. Chi Kung in Recovery will be an important resource for anyone wishing to learn about Chi Kung and practice this ancient art. Greg is a master teacher!"

Mel Pohl, MD, FASAM
Medical Director, Las Vegas Recovery Center

. . .

"Many people don't realize that the treasure of Chi Kung was almost lost due to 'political cleansing' and past masters keeping methods 'secret.' Kudos and much thanks to Greg Pergament for keeping a tradition that has been around for hundreds of years alive and captured in print. Chi Kung in Recovery is a practical and easy to understand book for anyone who is looking for alternative methods to help them through the 'crazy struggles of life.'"

Dashi Steven Baugh
Founder, Director, Master Instructor, and Pastoral Spiritual Counselor
Lohan School of Shaolin

. . .

"As an insight meditation teacher and ardent Chi Kung practitioner, I am particularly pleased that Greg has masterfully woven the arts of recovery, Chi Kung, and mindfulness into one inspiring book. I hope many people will take the opportunity to benefit from its healing practices."

Heather Sundberg
Certified Insight Meditation Teacher and Dharma Leader

. . .

CHI KUNG IN RECOVERY

Chi Kung

IN RECOVERY

Finding Your Way
to a Balanced and
Centered Recovery

Gregory S. Pergament

CENTRAL RECOVERY PRESS

LAS VEGAS

Central Recovery Press (CRP) is committed to publishing exceptional materials addressing addiction treatment, recovery, and behavioral healthcare topics, including original and quality books, audio/visual communications, and web-based new media. Through a diverse selection of titles, we seek to contribute a broad range of unique resources for professionals, recovering individuals and their families, and the general public.

For more information, visit www.centralrecoverypress.com.

Publisher: Central Recovery Press
            3321 N. Buffalo Drive
            Las Vegas, NV 89129

18 17 16 15 14 13   1 2 3 4 5

ISBN: 978-1-937612-41-2 (paper)
       978-1-937612-42-9 (e-book)

Cover and interior design by Sara Streifel, Think Creative Design
Illustrations by Gabby Gamboa

I dedicate this book

to the elimination of suffering

in all beings

without exception

欽定四庫全書

TABLE OF CONTENTS

*A **note to the reader**: To help you better understand the terminology in this book, a glossary has been included for your reference. Words that are included in the glossary are bolded the first time they appear in the text.*

PREFACE

I am a recovering addict, and I am a **Tai Chi** and Chi Kung practitioner and teacher—two paths that did not cross easily or simultaneously. Addiction, in all its blinding ferocity, brought me to my knees numerous times and finally to recovery some twenty-five years ago. Chi Kung didn't enter my life until another seven years later, through the practice of **Tai Chi Chuan**. I believe that twelve-step programs are marvelously effective at nurturing shattered lives into spiritual wholeness. The steps carefully lead the mind and the spirit into the process of recovery. However, twelve-step recovery rarely, if ever, mentions and does not address physical recovery from our disease, outside of the initial detoxification process. After all, the disease of addiction affects us physically, mentally, emotionally, and spiritually. Our energy or **"chi"** is primarily a physical attribute. There are few lifestyles I can think of that do more to deplete and dissipate our chi than active addiction. It is my hope that this book and the regular practice of Chi Kung will help restore your body to a harmonious state and expedite the healing process so that you can get on with the business of living, not dying.

I do have one caveat. Chi Kung is meant to be an enhancement to your recovery, not a substitute for it. There are no shortcuts. To recover from the disease of addiction we must work the steps, attend meetings, get and use a sponsor and, above all, stay clean from all mind- or mood-altering substances. This is my belief and the belief of thousands of my predecessors in twelve-step programs for whom recovery from active addiction became a reality.

ACKNOWLEDGMENTS

First and foremost I would like to thank Dashi Steven Baugh, founder and master of the Lohan School of Shaolin in Las Vegas, Nevada. Dashi Steve has been my Tai Chi Chuan and Chi Kung teacher and spiritual advisor since 1997. His dedication and determination inspired me to become the practitioner and teacher I am today.

I would also like to thank Tom and Darna Frank, my close friends and spiritual advisors. They have constantly encouraged me to see through the "smoke and mirrors" of everyday life and to focus on my vision.

I would like to send a great big spiritual hug to Pujari and Abhilasha for providing a safe and beautiful haven for me to recharge my spirit. Their gentle, yet resolute teachings have shown me what is important to value in life.

A great big hug to Kevin Griffin and Heather Sundberg, two of my teachers who have been the inspiration for my work in the very rich territory of Buddhism and the Twelve Steps.

I owe a debt of gratitude to the fellowship of Narcotics Anonymous for providing compassionate, nurturing rooms for this humble addict to come in from the cold.

A heartfelt thank you to the Las Vegas Recovery Center for trusting in me and in the benefits of Chi Kung for recovering addicts.

I would like to thank Eliza Tutellier, my loving and patient editor at CRP, who guided me through this process and crafted this book's final presentation, as well as Gabby Gamboa, for her painstaking work on the illustrations.

I also want to thank Casey Pergament for sharing me with Amy and Jennifer DePry. What a blessing it is to have such amazing daughters in my life.

And last, but certainly not least, I would like to thank my beloved partner, Leanne Earnest, for being my biggest fan. Her belief in me and my highest potential has been a beacon of luminous love and determination in my life.

INTRODUCTION

Chi Kung is an ancient Chinese healthcare system that integrates physical postures, breathing techniques, and focused attention. These three attributes make it an excellent complementary practice for anyone recovering from substance abuse and its physical, mental, emotional, and spiritual manifestations. Chi Kung creates an awareness of and influences dimensions of our being that are not part of traditional exercise programs. Most exercises do not involve the meridian system (used in **acupuncture**), nor do they emphasize the importance of mindful intent and breathing techniques in physical movements. When these dimensions are added, the benefits of exercise increase exponentially. The gentle, rhythmic movements of Chi Kung reduce stress, build stamina, increase vitality, and enhance the immune system. It has also been found to improve cardiovascular, respiratory, circulatory, lymphatic, and digestive functions. Consistent practice helps one regain a youthful vitality, maintain health into old age, and speed up recovery from illness. One of the more important long-term effects of Chi Kung is that it reestablishes the mind-body-spirit connection.

In late 2003, I was invited to an open house for Central Recovery's Las Vegas Recovery Center (LVRC). Since I am in recovery, I knew several of the staff there. During a casual conversation about what I had been doing lately, I naturally started talking about Tai Chi Chuan and Chi Kung and the benefits I was experiencing in my life. I had been practicing and teaching Chi Kung and Tai Chi Chuan at the Lohan School of Shaolin under the tutelage of **Dashi** Steven Baugh. They thought Chi Kung might be helpful to incorporate into the treatment program for their clients. After I explained a little more about Chi Kung, the smiles started to spread across their faces. The staff was particularly interested in the mind-body-spirit connection, which is exactly what recovery should entail. This was the beginning of my involvement with the "enhancement" program at Central Recovery.

In my Chi Kung teaching at LVRC I found it most useful to concentrate on the **Eight Section Brocade**. Eight refers to the number of individual exercises in the form that, when practiced together, impart an energetic quality in the body that is analogous to a piece of richly woven cloth (hence, "brocade"). It is a time-tested, safe system of Chi Kung. It is easy to learn and unparalleled when it comes to the general tonification of chi and improvement of one's health.

The age of the Eight Section Brocade is a much-debated subject. Liberal estimates guess that it is anywhere from 800 CE to a few thousand years old. For our purposes we just need to know that it is very old and that it predates modern Western medicine by a wide margin.

The Taoists, one of the primary practitioners of the Eight Section Brocade, had a different way of looking at life and one I think we would be well served to explore in modern society. Taoists were interested in cultivating harmony in all aspects of their lives. Their concept of the sky was that it was actually heaven. So as they walked upon the earth, they felt they were immersed in heaven. They believed that the human form was one of the major connection points between two powerful forces in nature: Heaven and Earth. During Chi Kung practice we become like batteries, simultaneously absorbing the energy from Heaven and Earth. This is the source for much of the stamina and vitality that ancient Taoists experienced through Chi Kung.

Today we are using this ancient system to help heal the shattered lives of those suffering from addiction. It is a perfect fit, especially when considering the ease with which it can be practiced, and what little strain it puts on the weakened condition of most newly recovering addicts.

As their bodies, minds, and spirits get stronger, recovering addicts become free to incorporate other healing modalities into their lives, while continuing to maintain a solid foundation in a twelve-step program. In this way they can become the healthy, vibrant, and happy beings they were always meant to be. Helping people become their true selves—physically, mentally, emotionally, and spiritually—is the aim of this book.

For recovering addicts, some of the biggest stumbling blocks in recovery, and in life more generally, seem to be our emotions. Many people have trouble coping with their feelings in a healthy manner, and addicts are especially prone to problems in this area. Quite simply, we are not used to addressing our emotions in a healthy way.

When we put down the substances we were abusing, we are confronted with the reality of our life experience in its entire splendor, both the good and the bad. The bad sometimes appears more prominent and causes us to falter in our recovery. Often these "negative" or should I say unpleasant emotions become so acute that they literally cause physical manifestations in our bodies. The Eight Section Brocade exercises are particularly effective in helping us neutralize these physical manifestations.

To help expedite healing, or to add another dimension to the process of Chi Kung, we can add a sacred sound or vibration to the exercises. Sound vibrations and their effect on healing have been known throughout human history. Most ancient cultures have used sound to heal, going back almost 40,000 years to the aboriginal people of Australia who were using the sound vibrations created by the **didgeridoo** to heal. Modern scientists are discovering that the sound vibrations from this ancient instrument are in alignment with modern sound therapy technology. Sound therapy all but disappeared in the West up until the 1930s when we discovered the ultrasound and its myriad healing properties. Ultrasound therapy has been used to break up kidney stones and even shrink tumors. The success of ultrasound technology has led to much research in the healing properties of infrasound and audible technologies.

Resonance may be the most important principle of sound healing. In healing, human beings' resonance can be described as the frequency of vibration that is most natural to a specific organ or system such as the liver, heart, or lungs. Where the resonance principle relates to cellular absorption of the healing sounds, this innate frequency is known as the prime resonance. In sound healing, these principles are used to re-harmonize cells that have possibly been imprinted with disruptive frequencies. Some imprints may have been the result of toxic substances, like drugs, emotional traumas, or pathogens.[1] In the context of the Eight Section Brocade Chi Kung exercises, we will use specific vocal sounds to help neutralize the physical effects of pain-infused emotions, help heal residual emotional baggage from our past, and prevent such emotions from dominating our lives in the present.

This book is primarily an instructional manual. It is designed for you to experience Chi Kung physically. For that to happen it will be necessary for you to read it a little differently from other books, stopping periodically to perform some of the exercises and meditations presented.

In addition to the Chi Kung exercises, there is a section on **mindfulness** with numerous guided instructions. As you embark on those, remember that mindfulness is an entirely experiential activity. You can read about mindfulness all you want, but until you practice it, the subtleties and the complexities will elude you.

If this book inspires you in any way, as I hope it will, I recommend that you seek out a teacher or other like-minded individuals to practice and learn with.

欽定四庫全書

My Story: From Addiction to Recovery—

DISCOVERING CHI KUNG

"If you can hear my voice, please raise your hand."

I recently attended a conference on Mindfulness in Las Vegas, Nevada. One of the workshops was led by Roshi Joan Halifax. She is a **Zen** priest at the Upaya Institute and Zen Center in Santa Fe, New Mexico. When the time came for her to begin her talk the room had grown quite noisy with numerous conversations of those attending. In a strikingly balanced and compassionate manner the Roshi brought the room to stillness and quiet, by simply speaking this phrase, "If you can hear my voice, please raise your hand." What affected me about this was how instinctual it was for her to act in this manner—gently, with such concern for everyone in attendance, yet with a motivation to move the event forward. This is the spirit in which I would like to present this section, "my story," as we say in the rooms of recovery. Often we present our story in a jarring or shocking manner. While some of what I will present may have that effect on readers, it is not my objective. Rather, "if you can hear my voice"—if you can relate—to any part of what I'm presenting, and you can acknowledge that recognition with a figurative "raising of your hand" in your heart, that is my intention. You see, there is more to "hearing my voice" than merely absorbing and processing sound waves moving through the air. It is indeed much deeper than that. It is a "quivering of the heart" in recognition of the suffering that has brought me to this day in my life.

So in the words of James McMurtry, "curl your lips around the taste of tears and the hollow sound that no one owns but you . . . ."[2]

This story is about a struggle, a war if you will, that occurred primarily in the space between my ears. It is the story of me at war with me, and as a result, at odds with almost everything I came in contact with. Through serious deliberate effort, I ended up creating a prison and a way of "death" (as opposed to life), that many people never escape from. Yet I did. I managed to crawl out of it on the other side, and for this I am deeply grateful. It was not easy. But like my **sponsor** used to say, "This is as easy as it gets for people like us."

I was born to a woman who was brave enough to walk away from an idyllic farm and a loving family in southeastern Pennsylvania. I say brave because she was the first and only one in a sibling group of seven to venture further than ten miles from the family farm. She was eighteen years old when she departed for Atlantic City, New Jersey, to get a summer job. She got a position working as a soft serve counter person at a custard stand on the infamous Atlantic City boardwalk. She met my father, or was seduced by him—the story varies—and became pregnant with yours truly. They married by the time my mother was three months pregnant.

I was born in the middle of a cold December night, and I was pissed. The reason I know this is thanks to my mother, who had the forethought of transcribing these sentiments in a baby journal. I was colicky, which meant I was in pain and cried a lot. My mother got some medicine from a doctor, gave it to me, and transcribed my reaction in my baby journal, "Boy, did he like it!" she wrote. The die was cast. I was three days old.

My earliest memories are of feeling dissatisfied. I don't ever remember feeling whole, complete, or happy. Don't get me wrong, there were many happy times, but they weren't frequent enough, and the ones I did have didn't last long enough. I knew my mother loved me, and I felt her unconditional love in the fabric of my being. With my father, however, it was different. He was a police officer, working rotating shifts, and he was gone a lot. As far as I was concerned this was fine. Especially as I got older, he was usually telling me to do things I didn't want to do or chastising me for things I did do. Frequently the incidents would be prefaced by the rhetorical question, "What's wrong with you?"

I do remember him being proud of me on occasions when he introduced me to someone he knew while we were together. I enjoyed being with him during these errands, but I don't remember him ever tossing me a ball, or teaching me how to play baseball or any other typical father-son type of activity. Our interactions consisted of me being along for the ride while he did whatever he wanted to do on that particular occasion, so our relationship was not what I would describe as close. I remember feeling as though his love depended on me acting or behaving in a certain way—and crying was not one of them. I remember being sensitive and feeling different because of this. It felt as though my emotions were right under my skin, ready to erupt in some dramatic display that was never considered justified or healthy by anyone who ended up being affected by it. I felt a strong lack of control because of this.

My brother was born when I was six years old. When my mother became pregnant with him I was not pleased. Up until that point I'd had my mother all to myself, and now I would have to share her. Not a virtue I was known for. I remember expressing this to her at some point and she held my face in her hands and told me, "Don't worry. You will always be my number one." I believed her. But I thought she meant her "favorite," and not just the numerical distinction. I also expressed some dissatisfaction about the possibility of receiving fewer gifts at Christmas because of my sibling. Again, she assured me that they would simply buy twice as much. I believed her. To say I was self-centered is an understatement, even at that young age.

I also remember always wanting to have a different kind of life. I wanted a mom who stayed home, wore an apron, baked cookies for no reason in a house with a picket fence, trees, and a dog yapping in a yard. Much like the lives I read about in the Dick and Jane books of the era. What I got was a three-story walkup apartment in a tenement full of winos, psychos, and other assorted ne'er-do-wells. My mom worked and left me with babysitters who treated me okay, but I was still pissed.

After my brother was born, we had a steady babysitter who watched my brother while my mom worked and I went to school. The babysitter liked my brother more than me and made no bones about expressing it. So I was pissed. Perhaps you are beginning to see a pattern. A pattern of nonspecific malaise; a pattern of never feeling satisfied; a pattern of dissatisfaction with my lot in life. Not so significant were it not for the very young age at which this feeling began. I wanted better or, more accurately, I was pissed that I didn't have better. All around me were kids living in worse environments than I, but I didn't care. I only knew what I wanted and what I didn't have, and this is how my life was lived for most of my childhood.

You can throw in some incidents of mischief, trespassing, and recklessness. It seems that with the participation of a loyal band of whatever misfits I was associating with at the time, I was always trying to change the way I felt. I was never comfortable in my own skin, always engaging in some reckless death-defying activity; like dodging waves on a jetty during a storm, or scouting abandoned buildings, or roaming into neighborhoods known to be hostile to outsiders. I was always on the lookout for that adrenalin rush, always the person who could be counted on to complete the dare. During this time I did manage to avoid drugs and the glue sniffing cliques that were common in our neighborhood. And I did well in school, taking pride in my ability to excel in most subjects.

Weekends, summers, and after school were spent exploring the alleys and backyards of all the apartment buildings that filled the blocks fronting the beach in the South Inlet of Atlantic City. Some summers my mom would send me to the farm in Pennsylvania to get a little country exposure for my developing city slicker psyche. I enjoyed those forays into farm life almost as much as my mom enjoyed the break from parenting. After all, she was a young mother. But even on the farm I felt different because my cousins called me a city slicker and my uncles treated me like I was weak or soft.

I wanted to be different from what I was. I wanted to look different. I wanted a different name. I wanted to be black. I wanted to be Puerto Rican. I wanted to be stronger. I wanted to be tougher. I wanted to be a star at sports, but I didn't want to practice. I fantasized about being the unrealized champion who emerges at the last minute and becomes the hero, winning the game and being showered with adulation and appreciation. I never felt contented with who I was, where I was, or what I was doing in my life. I lived in a world of fantasy.

In fifth grade I had a tyrant of a teacher. He was well-known as a rough-around-the-edges kind of guy. I did something in class that warranted him punishing me by having me write numerous repetitions of a particular sentence about what I had done. I cannot remember what the offense was, but the class was so surprised that I had done something wrong that they gasped in shock. I was mortified. As I started writing the sentences, the tears started to flow, followed by laughter from my classmates. The teacher eventually took pity on me and let me take my seat. This incident traumatized me to my core and further reinforced my belief that I was some sort of a sensitive, neurological freak or sissy. I told no one in my family about this event.

At the end of the school year, many months later, the teacher was shaking all the students' hands on their way out of the door and dispensing generous pleasantries all around. When he got to me he looked me straight in the eye, shook my hand, and said, "Greg, you are an excellent student and will go far in life if you can just learn to control your emotions." I deflated like a balloon stuck by a pin. Suddenly there were no more thoughts of summer vacation, no sunshine and swimming, no relief, just this overwhelming feeling of self-hatred and low self-esteem. I knew that I couldn't control my emotions, so I thought I would never be a success. I believed him. I was pissed. I crawled into a hole somewhere deep in my psyche and waited for the magic pill or magic method to arrive to transport me out of my emotional quagmire. I didn't have to wait very long, relatively speaking.

When the drugs and violence of our inner city lifestyle closed in on us—culminating in weekly stabbings and shootings in the numerous bars in our neighborhood—my mother thought it best to look for greener pastures. My father had found his greener pastures a few years earlier, and decided we wouldn't be part of his new life. That had been another bad day, where I had been pissed but also relieved in a way, since it meant that I would no longer have to endure his reproaches.

We moved to a "safer" neighborhood in Ventnor—Downbeach—they call it, but still on Absecon Island and still near the beach. I was entering seventh grade and immediately befriended two of the outcasts at the school. Go figure. I was still managing to sidestep drugs, with only a few forays with alcohol, one even cosigned by my mom. Her thoughts were, "At least he's not out somewhere doing God knows what!"

By that time I had noticed a pattern with my mother. I noticed that when she and her friends wanted to have a "good" time it always included alcohol. I also noticed when she had had a rough day or something was stressing her out, alcohol was the coping strategy. I filed this information away for future reference.

During that time my mother had been diagnosed with non-Hodgkins lymphoma. She hid the illness from my brother and me for a while, but she finally had to tell us about it when the treatments caused her to lose her hair. She spoke of it like it was a serious inconvenience. I don't know how my brother processed it, but I felt overwhelming dread. Life without the only person who really loved me was inconceivable. So I ignored it. And I was pissed.

In eighth grade, still hanging with the outcasts, our drugs of choice were mischief and gross vandalism. We destroyed things just for the rush, breaking windows just to hear the glass break. We threw eggs at passing cars. We terrorized anyone who appeared to have a better life than us, and that was a lot of people. We even called the police on ourselves, just for the fun of running from them. And the thing was, we were good at what we did, and always got away with it. It became our badge of honor in the neighborhood. Drug use was still curiously absent at that time of my life, but it was looming ever larger on the horizon.

In health class one day they passed around an anonymous survey that asked us various questions about drugs. It was 1971 and the establishment was trying to get a handle on how to deal with drugs, which were becoming a big problem in society. I remember the questions to this day: It asked if you knew anyone who took drugs—I answered yes. It asked if you ever took drugs—I answered no. It asked why—I answered, "I don't have to use drugs to enjoy life." Of course not, adrenalin was my drug, fueled by violent mischief and mayhem.

I don't know what happened exactly, but approximately six months later I was smoking pot and liking it. The magic pill had arrived. I made a decision that I would use pot recreationally and functionally. I would not let it interfere with my schoolwork. After all, I had plans for my life. I had no idea what those plans would be, but I knew I needed good grades, just in case. This actually worked for a while. I also decided to restrict my use to only marijuana, the "safe and natural" intoxicant. This restriction did not last long. My little group of outcasts did not take drugs so I hid my pot use from them. Also, I didn't want to get caught, so I mostly smoked by myself or with my uncle, my father's adopted brother who happened to be in college and was a pothead and a hippie. Not necessarily in that order. He was my idol. I thought, *See, he smoked pot all through college and he's doing just fine.*

This would not be the case with me, however. My efforts to restrict my use became increasingly troublesome. For one, I had the idea in the back of my mind that using was a way of celebrating or medicating, and in my world there was always something to celebrate or medicate over. So why not use all the time? Secondly, I started hearing about all sorts of exciting hallucinogens that really couldn't be much worse than weed now, could they? And I was off and running.

By now I had introduced one of the members of the outcasts to marijuana, and he loved it. The other members of our group faded from our lives amid much resentment and consternation. I had also started using with many of the established "heads" in our neighborhood. Many of them were dropouts who had a lot of experience with LSD, mushrooms, and other hallucinogens. I quickly joined in with them, but we were still careful to avoid the "bourgeois" drugs of our parents. Things like tobacco and alcohol, sleeping pills and tranquilizers. We had heard a higher calling and we were going to tear down the dried-up old status quo of our parents. All we really ended up doing was getting high a lot. This pattern lasted all through high school, from which I graduated with a 3.2 grade average and an SAT score of 1200—proof that my drug use was not interfering with my daily life functions. I was on my way to becoming a professional photographer. But not the type who photographs weddings and bar mitzvahs—something way cooler than that. In other words, nothing at all.

I moved out of my mom's apartment the summer after I graduated. This was motivated by a desire to get high whenever I wanted to, and not due to any maturing feelings of independence or desires to grow up. I also decided it would be best to take a year off and wait before jumping right into college, not least because my father had undermined my plans of going to school at the University of Florida in Gainesville. I had a great aunt who had promised to pay for my tuition when I came of age. My dad said he was not going to let her waste her money so I could go to Florida and get high. I was pissed, but subsequent events would show that it was not an unjustified concern on my father's part.

Many of the restrictions I had imposed on myself with my drug use began to dissolve once I got out on my own. My mother was growing increasingly ill and made more frequent trips to the hospital. A lot of the time I didn't bother to visit her. This, combined with the rapid disintegration of my coping strategies for controlling my drug use, meant I started using substances for the sake of forgetting, numbing, or not feeling. These substances included Quaaludes, downers, tranquilizers, alcohol, and painkillers, with a liberal sprinkling of meth and cocaine. All the hallucinogenic substances moved to the side as I developed my own method for coping with my mother's illness, my father's unavailability, and my basic disillusionment with life—such as I perceived it through dirty bathroom windows. I was spiraling out of control and exhibited only a modicum of restraint, just enough to keep myself out of jail and to stop just short of becoming too terribly addicted. The latter would soon change.

As my life unraveled I became very lonely and depressed, and I started to wonder where this path was leading me. I was working as a waiter in a hotel—sporadic and inconsistent work, but it paid in cash, which suited my lifestyle. I knew of this one guy who had that "dangerous" air around him, and was known to dabble in heroin. That was the last frontier as I saw it, the forbidden zone. It was the one boundary I had left that I hadn't violated . . . yet. So one day I asked him if he knew where I could get some "smack." He laughed and asked me if I had ever done it. I answered no but that I wanted to try it. He asked if I was sure and I answered yes. It turns out he did use heroin but presently he had a connection for something "better," liquid Dilaudid. He assured me it was measured, reliable, and just as good if not better than heroin. I was glad to hear the dosage was measured because I had some concern about the possibility of overdosing. This concern later proved to be portentous.

Being a novice, my friend "helped" me take the drug. When I did, I felt like I had died and gone to heaven. Everything was covered in velvet and bathed in a warm yellow light—after the initial vomiting, of course. I had finally found my magic pill. All those troublesome emotions dissolved in a spoonful of warm water. I was no longer pissed.

The path for me got very narrow, but not right away. I was careful to space out my usage because it was highly addictive stuff and very expensive compared to what I was used to spending on getting high. But soon I wouldn't care about the price or the addictive nature of the substance. I quickly learned how to fix myself and I remember when the thought came into my head that this was going to be bad, that this was how I would die someday. But the thought dissipated quickly.

My mother hardly saw me anymore and when I visited I was careful to wear long-sleeve shirts and never stayed too long. One morning I was sleeping in my friend's room in a boarding house—because my own room had no heat—and there was a knock on the door. It was a motorcycle cop. My friend started to panic. The cop asked for me by name. There was no dope left, we had made sure of that the night before, so I answered the door. Standing there was the same cop who had taken me for a ride on his motorcycle when I was six years old. He had a look of disgust on his face. "Let's go," he said, "your mom is really bad in the hospital."

My father had sent him to get me. I wondered how he had found me. I thought I was invisible. But my father was a cop and a good one. My mind was reeling from a confusing combination of heroin and fear. Fear that I was about to lose my mother and that no amount of dope could change that. At the hospital the entourage of relatives from Pennsylvania had gone to freshen up, so it was just me and dear old Dad. I had just checked in on Mom and she was—ironically— mumbling through her own opiate haze. I heard her say, "It's so funny. It's so funny," with a half smile on her face. These were the last words my mother would ever say to me.

We convened in the waiting room to give the medical staff space to attend to her. Dad decided to try and tell me, to somehow penetrate my heroin fog, that my mother would not be leaving the hospital this time. Suddenly a nurse came and touched my shoulder. "She's gone," the nurse said. I ran to the room and hugged my mom's still warm body, felt the weight of her emaciated frame, and cried.

I was really pissed now. I noticed a while later that my emotions had crept through the narcotics—I wasn't numb anymore, but not for lack of trying. I was hollow, alone, and consumed with self-pity and anger. I briefly contemplated returning to Mom's apartment to rifle through her opiate collection, rationalizing that she really didn't like them and sure didn't need them now. Visiting relatives made this shameful escapade impossible. So instead I hit the streets. Ripping and running on a tear beyond anything I had ever attempted before. It was so bad that I left all the funeral arrangements to my relatives; everything, even the disposal of her effects and the auctioning of her furniture.

A few days after the funeral I totaled another car, managing to break my hand so badly they had to put pins in it. With nowhere to turn, I went back to rural Pennsylvania so my relatives could take care of me. After a few weeks of staring out at the snow and desolate landscape of winter, my uncles were talking about getting me a job at one of the numerous factories in the area. I had to move fast. I called a friend back in New Jersey to complain of my predicament, and he agreed to let me come live with him and his mother for a while. So I did. And I was off again. Dope became my lover, my obsession, my life.

One time a girlfriend caught me using. The next day she asked if she could watch and I said sure. *This was great*, I thought. *Now I don't have to hide it from her*. She watched and then commented that I loved that dope more than her. She said she could tell by my face. I embraced her, held her face in my hands, looked her straight in the eyes and said, "Don't be ridiculous, that's not true. But just don't ever try to come between us." And I meant it. I had found what I had been missing my entire life: complete control over my emotions. The problem was that, in turn, I had to give complete control to those substances. But at that point I didn't care. That would change.

I started to accumulate car accidents. By the time I got clean I counted thirteen accidents—four of those accidents totaled the car. I had a moment of clarity at one point and made a decision that may have saved my life. I decided to stop driving. My insurance premiums had increased to an unmanageable rate anyway and I had no car. So I placed my license in a drawer and left it there for eight years. It never dawned on me to stop using, or even to slow down. That was not negotiable. Besides, it was the driving that was the problem, not the using. It's not that I completely stopped driving either, but I did curtail it drastically. Not because of any great concern for my own life, but because I knew it was only a matter of time before I would kill some soccer mom in a van full of kids. Even I didn't want to take that risk.

That I managed to avoid prison was most likely due to a combination of my father's influence, police apathy for common junkies, and my unremarkable criminal exploits. Whatever the reason, I am grateful, because I would have lacked the temperament for prison life.

I became a master of substitution during that tumultuous period, constantly switching drugs and experimenting with different combinations to avoid addiction. It rarely worked and, ultimately, only prolonged the suffering.

One day I met a woman who used like I did. We fell in love, got high as hell, had a baby, got married, and lived happily ever after . . . well, not quite. I remember thinking when we met that this was great—not only would I not have to hide my using, we could use together! But it wasn't great. It was a nightmare.

We had two habits to contend with. We started to get strung out on a consistent basis. It was a bit like the movie, *Sid and Nancy*, without the music. I was starting to rack up overdoses. After the first one, I felt as though I was invincible. I walked out of the hospital and into the nearest bar, where my friends and girlfriend were crying over their drinks, imagining my death. I didn't understand what all the fuss was about.

I began overdosing all over town and came dangerously close to dying several times. Yet I didn't, and my reputation grew. Around the drug houses and projects I frequented I became known as "The Dead White Boy," and many people wouldn't sell to me because of it. Friends would be reluctant to let me into their homes and I could only use their restroom if I left the door open. They didn't want to have to explain a corpse to the police. People were starting to look at me with that faraway look of pity. Everyone was waiting to get the call that I had finally died.

Then my girlfriend became pregnant. She had to stop using and begged me to do the same. I told her that I agreed to be a father but I never agreed to stop using! Don't be ridiculous. I went wild. Now I only had one habit to contend with. I was on easy street. I drove her crazy with my aberrant behavior; in constant conflict with her innate desire to provide a good home for our child. Our child, a beautiful baby girl, was born healthy, and so it was business as usual for us. We somehow managed to provide a relatively nice home for our daughter, "nice" at least as far as junkies are concerned.

As I mentioned before, my criminal abilities were unremarkable, so stealing wasn't a very reliable way to support my addiction. As a result, I always held a job. I knew I needed a steady income to stay as high as I was accustomed to. Most people work in order to live the lifestyle they are accustomed to. My particular lifestyle was drugs, period.

I got high at my hotel job, of course, and created a small inner circle of junkies whom I could rely on and use with at work. One of them got a hold of a particularly strong batch of dope one time. It was Thanksgiving Eve and we were set to visit my girlfriend's parents the next day for supper.

The phone rang; it was "the good dope" calling. He was at work, the same hotel where I worked, but this was my day off. He wanted me to do him a favor, and I said no problem, as I wanted another bag of that good stuff. He said to come over, despite the fact that I was already plenty high; despite the fact that my girlfriend was waiting for me; despite the fact that I had a beautiful two-year-old daughter; despite the fact that Thanksgiving with the folks was the next day; despite everything—because this was "the good dope." I did it anyway.

I woke up in the ladies' room with two crews of ambulance personnel, security, food and beverage supervisors, and other assorted people of authority. They were asking me what I had taken. I asked them where the guy went, the guy who held me down and injected drugs into my arm. Everybody had a good laugh at that one. And then one female EMT looked me right in my desperate pin-sized pupils and said, "Greg, tell us what you took so we can help you." I told them and they did.

Thanksgiving was rather unpleasant the next day, as I tried to shake off the effects of the Narcan that was used to save my life the night before and hide the bruises on my hands as I reached for the mashed potatoes. Meanwhile, my girlfriend glared at me for my inability to stay out of emergency rooms. She was not mad because I used, only about the fact that I kept almost dying. I fell asleep on the sofa while the family gathered and my daughter played.

The hotel brought me in to continue their investigation. I had already called EAP (Employee Assistance Program) and was set to go to rehab and clean up my act. I even went to a twelve-step meeting. Granted I was loaded when I went and had a pint of vodka in my pocket, but I went. The New Jersey State Police had another idea. They wanted to know who was in this "inner circle" of junkies they had heard about. They had an idea that I wasn't alone during my overdose. I tried to appeal to them and said that I was a loner and just wanted to change my life now. They didn't believe me, or if they did they didn't care. They wanted an informant. I told them I wasn't interested. They said I was uncooperative. The EAP lady called the next day to tell me the rehab offer was off the table, as was my job. In addition, they had instituted proceedings to revoke my license to work in any casino.

Naturally, I was pissed. So I used. Mostly alcohol for a while, but I eventually returned to heroin. The legal proceedings were taking a long time. I was grateful. I was working in another hotel while I waited for the ax to fall.

I had a friend at my new job who used crack. He was very obvious about his using and one day management pulled him into the office and told him he had to go to rehab. I asked him what that meant, and he said it meant he had to stay clean forever if he wanted to keep his job. I remember telling him, "That sucks." I was grateful that it wasn't me. I was drinking copious amounts of alcohol at that time and backing it up with liberal use of dope.

On Memorial Day of 1988—something about me and holidays, I guess—I was in a bar drinking when my girlfriend walked in, carrying our daughter. We started to argue, and I took our daughter in my arms and said I was taking her home. On the way out the door I snatched the keys to the car she had "borrowed" off the bar. At the door I met my neighbor who was a using buddy of mine. I asked him if he wanted to get high. He said yes and asked if I had wheels. I jingled the keys and said, "I do now."

The third car we tried worked and so we were off. We headed to the projects in a stolen car with my daughter. We arrived at a glass-strewn empty lot near the projects where I was to wait. I did. It was late. My daughter was asleep with her head on my lap. A clear thought entered my drunken haze, *This is not cool . . . this is messed up*, as I lovingly gazed down at my daughter. Even with that feeling of love flooding through me and knowing that what I was doing was extremely wrong, I was unable to stop the course of events.

My friend came back and said, "I can't find anyone. It's too late." The universe, spirit, God, karma, or whatever was trying to intervene. I circumvented that and said, "You better find it or I'm not driving you home." He did. We went home. The dope was stamped "Last Stop." That was the last bag of dope I ever took and the last time I almost died. Only this time my girlfriend overdosed, too.

I woke up in the ER, hooked up to Narcan once again. I looked over and saw my girlfriend. I told her to get up, that we had to leave or we would be arrested. She started to cry, told me we almost died, and showed me her chest. Her entire upper torso was covered in black and blue marks from the CPR. I laid back down on my gurney and tried to formulate another plan. We didn't know where our daughter was. We didn't know our legal status. But, miraculously, we were alive.

We were released early the next morning and went home. We found out that the police had delivered our daughter to her maternal grandparents. It turned out that one of the police officers' wives knew us and convinced her husband to have mercy on our daughter and to not put her in the system. For that I am eternally grateful. The police contacted us and told us we were still under investigation and that charges may be pending.

The fact that we survived did not go unnoticed by me. My dying was one thing, but both of us leaving our beloved daughter was too much. My girlfriend was very depressed, and I was in a daze. Unfortunately, I was desensitized to the overdosing process as that had been my sixth hospital-treated overdose. So I went back to work. After all, the show must go on, right?

When I returned home that night the house was dark. I had no keys, because the police had taken them, along with my ID, my phone book, and numerous other items, though I couldn't figure out why. I had to break into my own house. Once inside I was greeted by a "Dear John" letter: "Dear Greg, I love you but I can't go on living this way." I was devastated. I *knew she was no good*, I thought. I *knew she would leave me when I was down*! She was a junkie, like me. What does it say about a person when fellow junkies no longer want to be around you?

I was pissed, so I used. I ranted and raged. I plotted and schemed with my using buddy about how we would conquer the world. How we would take advantage of anyone who dared to cross our path. It was a lot of sick drug-addled rambling that ended one day with me staring out of my kitchen window as dawn smeared the day awake, and suicide sounded like a mighty good idea. That was it; the day I'd always known would come, my last day on earth. I would check out, and the world would keep on spinning without me.

I fantasized about how much better off my daughter would be with a dad who would take care of her. And how my girlfriend would have a husband who cared for her and who would never let her down. My friends would read about my death in the papers and shake their heads at the memory of my crazy life. It was a really sick, melodramatic, soap-opera type head-trip, and suddenly I got scared. Staring out of that window with tears rolling down my cheeks I started to shake. I mean really tremble. I was trembling in fear of what I was about to do in my desperate condition.

Just then, a thought entered my head—one solitary idea shot straight from the divine. *Why don't you try getting clean first*? It was the only thing I had never tried since my whole miserable trip began. *If that didn't work I could always resort to plan* B, I thought. I wiped my tears and reached for the phone. I called my stepsister, the only person I knew who had used like I had and who was now staying clean in a twelve-step program. I broke down when she answered the phone.

She told me to come down to her house, have dinner, and then she would take me to a meeting. She asked me if I had anything in the house, I said "No." I hung up the phone, downed the three beers I lied about, and started to walk to her house. Once there I was unable to eat and the withdrawal was starting to seep through the effects of the beer. My sister was having trouble getting us a ride so I graciously offered to wait until tomorrow, stating that I wasn't feeling so good anyway. My sister, a barroom brawler of mythic proportions, ordered me to sit still as she called for a cab. Thirty-five dollars lighter, my sister escorted me into my first twelve-step meeting.

My disease was acutely aware of the potential for change this indicated, and it started to react strongly. I was shaking and sweating and could barely walk or speak. Yet the people I met there were genuinely happy that I had come. It had been a long time since people—friends or family—had reacted this way to my appearance on their doorstep. Cautious resignation was the best I ever got in these later days.

So I walked in and sat down, consumed with a fear that was as unfounded as it was pronounced. I realize now that it was my disease. The jig was up. This was the beginning of a powerful transformation that would turn the tables on my active addiction in a way I would have never thought possible. People like me just didn't get better, they died, period, or went to prison for a long time. This was the lie I believed. My twelve-step fellowship showed me how to dispel that lie and how to live a life free from active addiction in all its various forms. I cannot tell you what was said at that first meeting, but I remember the smiles, the welcome hugs, and the enthusiasm of addicts who wanted nothing more than for me to get clean and stay in recovery. And they had an unwavering faith in my ability to do so, long before I thought it possible.

One crazy individual, who became my first sponsor, offered my sister and me a ride home. At one point we stopped by the ocean, so he and my sister could talk. She had a lot of drama going on and he was willing to help her sort it out. This was a little odd to me but I was along for the ride. As we sat there we must have appeared suspicious because a police car rolled up on us from behind and I instinctively stiffened with fear, then relaxed and started to laugh and smile. Dave asked me what was so funny and I replied that I couldn't remember an interaction with the police that didn't involve the possibility of me going to jail. I was free from that. I had experienced my first taste of freedom in recovery and it was only my first day. It would get better, much better in fact, and freedom would spread into all areas of my life—and not just in the legal sense.

The next day I realized it may have been a mistake to let Dave drive me home, as now this maniacal twelve-step pirate knew where I lived and would be stopping by to shanghai me to meetings whenever the urge came over him, which was every day and often several times a day! I would not be able to slip through the cracks with this guy standing watch. I am grateful, to this day, for Dave's commitment to carrying the message of recovery to me.

I asked Dave to sponsor me. He was around every day anyway. What attracted me to him as a sponsor—besides the scar running down his left arm from his bicep to the middle of his forearm—was his unshakeable faith in my ability to get clean, stay clean, and live a life beyond my wildest dreams. He was emphatic about this and talked about it constantly. I remember thinking that I was getting "brainwashed." This bothered me until I realized that my brain could probably use a little washing. I needed to develop a new way of thinking about my life and about the world in which I lived.

Fortunately, the Twelve Steps are well-adapted to facilitating just that kind of mental transformation. I began to notice that people in the meetings seemed to be happier than I was, more grateful than I was, and much calmer than I was. It was the steps. They were writing and working on one or another of the Twelve Steps and were experiencing the kind of life I wanted. I had already experienced a tremendous amount of relief by just identifying as an addict and finally understanding what my problem was and why I had felt different and unsatisfied virtually my entire life, even before using drugs.

I was a good follower. After all, isn't that what addicts do? We see someone doing something or taking something that might be of use to us, in our warped way of seeing things, and we copy it. I was not the first person to figure out drugs were a strategy for coping with what I saw as the intolerable condition of life. I saw others doing it and followed suit. It was the same for my recovery. I saw others getting more out of it and started copying them. And voilà, I started to feel, and act, healthier. I started discovering who I was and what my limiting beliefs were that kept me caught in so many vicious circles.

Sponsorship was rather vigorous and unyielding in those days, so when I went against my sponsor's advice for reuniting with my addict girlfriend and our child, he cut me loose. His exact words were, "If you want to run your own recovery, you don't need me. You're on your own." Wow. I thought it a tad harsh, but I stayed clean out of resentment for a few months because he told me I would get high and die if I brought my girlfriend back. To be fair, it was very difficult when she came back, and I did come very close to relapsing a few times, but I didn't.

About two weeks into my recovery, my friend from work who had gone to rehab came back. He walked into the restaurant with his eyes clear and wide open. I greeted him and we chatted about his experience. I asked him what he was doing after work. I saw him stiffen at the expectation of an offer to use. Instead, I asked him if he wanted to go to a meeting. He was shocked. He smiled and we hugged and I gave him the short version of what had happened to me while he was away. That's the way the disease works. In two short weeks I went from pity for my friend for having to stop using, to begging for relief from my own addiction. That is how quickly this disease can unravel your life. And if you're lucky, blessed, or in some cases, forced, you make it into the rooms of a twelve-step program.

I have to say that I was struggling with the "God" word in those early days. It wasn't that I didn't believe in God, so much as I was pissed at God. For a long period of time I wouldn't even say the word. If I was reading aloud at a meeting and I came to the word "God," I would just say "blank." Some addicts would laugh and tell me to "keep coming back." One day, with a sponsor's help, I came to realize that it was a just a word used to describe the cause for the effects I was already experiencing in my life. And I really did get to believe in a God of my own understanding. This principle is absolute and without any catches, and it's a very important thing to realize if you want to stay in recovery in a twelve-step fellowship.

I made it to meetings on a regular basis, just like the suggestions advise. I eventually chose another sponsor, and the first thing he told me was that he didn't agree with what my previous sponsor had done when he let me go. There was some controversy and a lot of strong opinions in those early days, but somehow I stayed, even when my head told me to leave. The one thing I knew without a doubt was that I had no idea how to stay in recovery on my own, and these people, as crazy as they were sometimes, obviously did. I had nowhere else to turn. It *was* the Last Stop for me—ironic, given the stamp on that last bag of dope I had used. If my chosen twelve-step program wasn't going to work, there was a strong likelihood that I would die in the horrors of active addiction. I wasn't going to make it to prison or to an institution. Sooner or later someone would run instead of calling an ambulance, or the ambulance would get a flat tire, or any number of possibilities in the balance of which my life would hang. Either way, I figured that my luck, my karma, or whatever you want to call it, was very close to running out.

Fortunately, I did not have to run that trail to the bitter end. I found a way, as have countless others before me and after. And just like the Basic Text says, "It is available to us all."[3] There are no poor unfortunates in my twelve-step program. It is a program that is given freely, and anyone can recover based on a desire to do so. The trick is getting through those doors during those small windows of opportunity that can be so elusive to us addicts. Many slip back out again, and again, and again, and again, believing that the program won't work for them, or simply not wanting to put in the necessary work.

Personally, I knew that the program worked. Early on, I witnessed miraculous transformations. People who I would have never guessed could get and stay drug-free were doing so, and showing me the way. I did think for a brief period of time that I would mess up the program, or that I would somehow overanalyze it and end up disqualifying myself, and in the process "embarrass" my entire twelve-step fellowship. Other addicts convinced me that this was my disease trying to put me on the outside once again and distance me from the program. So I stayed put.

It's not that I haven't been close to relapse dozens of times. Dangerously close in fact. But I just followed the few simple suggestions that were made available to me from that first day. I made it to a meeting and/or I called another addict and talked about it. I read the chapter in the Basic Text on "Relapse and Recovery" until the pages wore thin. And the impulse to use would pass. And slowly but surely, over time, my instinctual, habitual reactions to situations started to change. As I gradually inclined my mind, situation by situation, into another, more wholesome direction, I became less inclined toward using, toward violence and avoidance. Instead, I started to walk through pain, to not use no matter what, and to confront situations with my head held high, even when fear was nipping at my heels.

I had created some considerable wreckage with my behavior in active addiction and, like all recovering addicts, the time came for me to face up to it. I found out that the State of New Jersey was not all that impressed with my newfound abstinent way of life. You see, many people still believe in that age-old lie that "once an addict always an addict," and many of those people work at agencies that have the power to seriously affect what you do in your life. This is just a fact of life, but here we are, twenty-four years later, and a lot has changed. Thanks mostly to the countless recovering addicts who have managed to arrest the active part of their addiction and become productive members of society over these intervening years.

The Division of Gaming Enforcement was in the process of revoking my gaming license, which was a requirement to work in any capacity in a casino hotel during the late eighties. I had been in recovery for nine months by the time the hammer fell. I had collected as much documentation as I could, attesting to the change in my lifestyle. I had letters from EAP counselors, an outpatient program, and even an administrative law judge who had dismissed the case against me. I was home free, or so I thought. As I stood in front of the five judges who made up the Casino Control Commission—I mean, five judges—I pled my case without a lawyer, since I lacked the funds to hire one.

They listened attentively and then started to ask questions. They said the administrative law judge had erred. They wanted to know what "guarantee" I could provide to assure them that I wouldn't use narcotics again or, furthermore, overdose in one of their bathrooms. I told them that all I had was my word and my intention to leave that way of life far behind me. I added that I had never been as far from drugs in my entire life as I was at that moment. I also offered to submit to random drug testing. They informed me smugly that they were not in the drug-abuse monitoring business, and voted unanimously to revoke my license for life.

I was devastated, deflated, and whirling in disbelief. The only upside was that they weren't putting me in jail. But they had effectively revoked my ability to support myself and my family in Atlantic City. The only worthwhile waiter jobs were in the casinos. The severity of their decision was unheard of; I knew of convicted felons who were working in the hotels. They obviously wanted to set an example with me, especially since they had labeled me uncooperative in their undercover operation. The paper they gave me stated I could reapply for a license in five years.

My head was spinning as I left the building. I walked into a coffee shop and, lo and behold, there was one of my using buddies, smiling as he sat in between two women of dubious moral character who were also smiling. He invited me over and asked if I wanted to go party with them. It was an enticing offer, especially considering the recent turn of events. I looked him in the eye, told him what had just happened to me, and left with a cup of coffee in my hand, headed to a noon twelve-step meeting.

I went into that meeting and broke down. I cried and complained, stomped my feet and hung my head. The people there loved me up. They cared. They told me everything would be all right. I looked at them in disbelief. After the meeting a woman came up to me and said the small restaurant she was working in was looking for another waiter. It turned out the owner knew my family and he had a son who was also in recovery. He hired me. I had only been unemployed for three days.

This is just one of many such situations where I had a choice, and where, more often than not, the wrong one would look quite tantalizing. My job is to see that clearly, and to consistently make the better choice. That is the bedrock of recovery: choosing not to use no matter the circumstances. But without the support of other recovering addicts it is virtually impossible to do on a regular basis.

In the beginning the desire to use was strong. It was all I thought about; I just didn't act on it. Other addicts told me to just say the Serenity Prayer whenever I thought about using, so I basically walked around saying the Serenity Prayer all the time in my head, without the "God" word, of course:

> "Whatever is up there, grant me the serenity
> to accept the things I cannot change,
>
> The courage to change the things I can,
>
> And the wisdom to know the difference."

This is such a simple but powerful statement of intention regardless of what your concept of God is. However, for me, initially nothing was happening. Weeks and weeks and still no relief from my addicted mind-stream. I had spent years cultivating a particular pattern of destructive thought and now I wanted relief. Finally, one night as I cried alone in my bedroom consumed with the overwhelming desire to change the way I felt, I collapsed in surrender. I begged, "Whatever is up there, take away my obsession to use or take me from this life." I was done. I couldn't take it any more.

In fact, I could and would take much more. The Twelve Steps eventually gave me power over the disease of addiction. I was surprised that soon after that fateful night, I woke up and went about my daily business, and at one point realized that I had been awake for half the day and hadn't thought about using yet. It was better than Christmas. I couldn't wait to get to a meeting and to tell everybody that they were right. They just smiled and clapped their hands, taking joy in my newfound hope. Of course the desire to use would still come and go, but now I had hope. Now I knew, from experience, that it was a passing phenomenon and not a permanent mental state. It would pass. I didn't have to act on any habitual thought that came into my mind, no matter how powerful or permanent it seemed. Plus, it meant that everything else they were telling me about recovery had the potential to be true, too.

So I stayed clean, worked my program, hung out with recovering addicts and my life rolled along smoothly. We had a lot of fun along the way. I thought that people who stopped using walked around in this dull and boring life, like a bunch of emotionless zombies. Nothing could be further from the truth. We bowled together, laughed together, ate meals together, celebrated holidays together, traveled together, and managed to help others. My life had purpose. This desperate, hope-to-die dopefiend had found a way to transform all of that adversity into a lantern of hope and inspiration for others coming up behind him. It was a miracle, to be sure.

And then the years started to accumulate. I became a loving father, a loving supportive husband, and a son my father could be proud of. That's right, that policeman father and I actually developed a close, albeit long-distance, relationship. Laughing and chatting about our lives, with me no longer a constant drain on finances and emotions. And when he became sick and eventually died of cancer, I was there to comfort him, to hug him, to love him, and to let him know in his passing that I would be okay, that I would stand in this world as a man of substance and value.

He used to tease me about a twelve-step H&I (Hospitals and Institutions) commitment that I carried into a prison for a few years. He told me, coming from his slanted police point of view, that I was wasting my time. That convicts just go through those motions to get out early or to pass the time inside. I told him to remember the times when he thought I would die from my addiction and when he believed there was nothing he could do to stop it. I told him that this is what I did to stop it.

I made amends to him one day for all the harm I had done to him. We stood in a room in the Tropicana Hotel in Atlantic City, hugging and crying as the sun glinted off the ocean far below us. As tears ran down his face, he looked at me and said, "It's easy to forgive you for the things you've done, because of my work I know that not many of you ever get better. And if that prison shit you do is part of this thing, then keep on doing it." And I did, for four years.

After his passing, his best friend (my uncle) asked me if I knew how proud my dad was of me. Had he ever told me? I said no. My uncle said my dad was proud of me and would talk about my road to recovery all the time. If someone came to him with a son or daughter caught in addiction he would offer me as a story of hope to them. The lie that we do not recover was dying. People no longer believe that death is the inevitable result of addiction. Death is a distinct possibility, but not inevitable.

My concept of a higher power has evolved over the years. This God that I began to petition and rely on for help on a daily basis evolved into a quietly divine presence that pervades all things like energy. It is still a great mystery to me, but now I feel it. I feel it in the tall trees, and the blowing wind. I feel it in the crashing waves, and the utter silence of a desert sunset. The work is here within me, to offer up thanks on a daily basis for this reprieve we call recovery. I give thanks for this life, for all its twists and turns, the blessings, and the lessons. I am responsible for my life and how I live it today. What happens in my life is no longer someone else's fault. I can no longer use addiction as an excuse for my unwholesome decisions.

My recovery has been firmly rooted in the realization that I am an addict and that other people can help me live a life free of substances. I devised a God of my own understanding in which to ground the whole process. I carried on by completing a searching and fearless inventory of myself that laid bare my patterns of behavior, the good and the not-so-good. I personally did not gain tremendous freedom from this step, but it did reveal the true nature of my addiction. Then

I shared it with someone—all my deep, dark secrets—in one long night, and I cried and laughed and realized that I am not alone and that I am not all those terrible things I had done.

I have been able to redesign myself, and the redesigning process began with the subsequent steps, where I took a hard look at the behaviors and motives behind my use of substances. My defects of character amounted to a dysfunctional system I had created for myself as a failed strategy for coping with life. Ultimately it both led to, and was a product of, my active addiction. It was like the alpha and the omega: Some of those defects were present before drug use and some grew out of it, but all of them had to go.

This is where God and I bumped heads. I thought God would simply lift those things from me. Remove them like the step says when I ask him to. I realized that it was more complicated than that. I had work to do. I had to apply effort toward changing my behavior in connection with those things, over and over again, and then my mind would gradually be less inclined toward those shortcomings. I had to break the habit with my unhealthy behaviors just like I had to break the habit of active using by not picking up drugs. The fabric underlying these changes, the courage and willingness to follow through with them, would come from my higher power. And that process continues to this day.

After cleaning up some of my behavior in this way it was time to make amends to all the people I had harmed. Without the grounding presence of a sponsor and a loving God, this can be a very slippery slope. I avoided a lot of pain by heeding my sponsor's advice about when and to whom to make amends. Well, I didn't avoid all the pain of course. I had one person tell me by proxy what I could go do to myself. But I had plenty of support to help me through that and, ultimately, I felt tremendous relief after this step. Freedom was occurring.

The remaining steps are my maintenance steps where I look at my intentions and motivations and make the necessary corrections, especially in situations where I am wrong. I pray and meditate on a daily basis and as a result, on most days, I am mindful of what is going on and the part I play within that. And then of course I share my recovery. I share and teach these things, these principles of life and recovery—these steps—to other people. Not all of those I share these gifts with have to be addicts these days either. There is plenty of suffering going on within as well as outside of the realm of addiction, and I have grown to include and respond to whomever reaches out for help.

Chi Kung entered my life when I had been in recovery for about seven years. I started to get curious about Tai Chi Chuan, a moving meditation/martial art form, and I was looking for something physical to do in my recovery. I heard about an eight-week class being held at a community center a few towns over and soon found that you don't learn much about Tai Chi in eight weeks. So I continued on. It was the **"Wu" style of Tai Chi** that I was learning. I also learned a little Chi Kung, which was designed to help one's Tai Chi practice.

Frankly, at that time, I didn't care for Chi Kung. It was very slow and there didn't seem to be a lot going on with it. I was more interested in the martial arts aspect and, besides, I was having trouble feeling this mysterious "chi" they were always talking about. Tai Chi was a nice way for me to do something physical while in recovery. I didn't yet fully realize its value in this area and was just looking at it as something I did in addition to my recovery. It was not yet incorporated into my recovery.

I continued with two different teachers in Wu style for a year and had just finished learning the "Wu 108 set," a very long, traditional form of Tai Chi. Our teacher was very systematic and wouldn't teach us any weapons or push hands exercises until we had finished learning the form, could demonstrate it in front of the class, and take criticism from each and every one of our classmates. Our master was Eddie Wu from Toronto. He would come down occasionally to beat us up and teach us the finer points of this very martial arts style of Tai Chi. Then my daughter, my wife, and I moved to Las Vegas, Nevada. There was no Wu style here, so I practiced what I had learned and waited. I wouldn't have to wait long.

One morning it was slow at work so I was practicing some simple Chi Kung exercises, and a Chinese lady I worked with noticed it. "You know Chi Kung!" she exclaimed. I said I knew a little from back in New Jersey. She said she had something for me and would bring it the next day. She brought me a simple flyer for Tai Chi, Chi Kung, and Kung Fu classes being held on a veranda in Chinatown. So I went to check it out. There was a small crowd of people watching this Native American guy with long hair teach a small class of avid students. During one of the breaks the teacher looked straight into my eyes and nodded. I walked over to him and began to ask questions.

We hit it off immediately. He was friendly and approachable yet moved with power and confidence. He said he did not teach Wu style, in fact no one in Las Vegas did. The only Wu teacher he knew of was in LA. He told me I would like **"Chen" style**, which he taught. I balked because I had heard about Chen. It is known to be a difficult form with a lot of jumping and stomping, fast and slow parts. He also taught **"Yang" style Tai Chi Chuan** and said I could start there.

I did and have continued training with him to this day. Dashi Steven Baugh has taught me to love Chi Kung and Tai Chi Chuan. From the beginning he had an engaging way of describing the various forms he taught, and he always emphasized the advantages Chi Kung would bring to one's martial art and to one's overall health. And he was right—I do like Chen style. It is a very energetic form of Tai Chi that really gets the blood flowing. Most importantly, I am able to appreciate the value of Chi Kung for my life and my recovery through Dashi Steve's expanded way of teaching.

Over time and as I deepened my practice, I was able to realize the force of chi in my body and in my environment. Active addiction has a way of cutting us off from ourselves and our true nature, and with Chi Kung I was able to reconnect, in a meaningful way, with my body and its inherent energy and qualities. This awareness translated to my environment as well, and I was able to feel the energetic qualities of my surroundings, both the good and the not-so-good. Gradually, I started to gravitate toward the more wholesome places of energy and to abandon the unwholesome. This was quite the opposite of what happened during my active addiction, where I seemed to be inexplicably drawn to the negative and destructive forces in the world. Unfortunately, as addicts we can continue in this manner even in recovery. It's only when we gather wisdom and awareness and are able to notice the difference and make the necessary choices that we no longer feel drawn to frequent places where the energy is not supportive of our best interests. And, in time, we can become vigilant in this area and consequently avoid a lot of unnecessary discomfort in our recovery. It is kind of like bringing the concept of "avoiding people, places, and things" into a sometimes subtle energetic awareness. Chi Kung is especially good at cultivating awareness of qualities of energy.

Having said that, I was by no means a quick study in these energetic arts; in fact, it took me an inordinately long time to be able to manifest or feel this energy in my body. Normally the hands are the first place one senses chi. It feels like heat, tingling, vibrating, pulsing, or trembling. It usually starts in the hands, feet, or face, but the sensation can travel throughout the body.

I was attending class regularly and practicing diligently, but I couldn't feel anything. I asked Dashi Steve what I was doing wrong. He said everyone is different to a degree. Everyone experiences different life circumstances that sometimes create energetic blockages and stagnations in the body. The exercises were working deep inside my body and along channels that I was not yet sensitive enough to detect. He added that I was a "special case." Because of the years spent in active addiction, I had blockages and stagnations that may have been more pronounced for me than for the average person. This made sense to me because active addiction is about not feeling, not integrating. It is about desensitizing, and basically cutting oneself off from life.

So with Dashi's patient guidance, I continued to practice. And lo and behold, one day I felt the sensation of chi flood into my hands. It felt like warm syrup flowing into my fingertips. I became very excited and reported this to Dashi who simply smiled and said, "Good." My practice gathered momentum after that, and I managed to keep up a regular practice in order to keep the chi flowing. This is necessary because our lifestyles are such that, even without active addiction, we continuously dissipate chi and create stagnations in our everyday life. We can limit the effects of this by practicing Chi Kung and adopting some of the life changes I discuss in this book. Things like nutrition, proper rest, healthy sexual practices, and spending time in nature.

Chi started flowing more smoothly in my body and I experienced an increase in vitality and stamina. In addition, I now get sick much less frequently, and when I do it doesn't last as long as it used to.

These are all positive, wholesome benefits of Chi Kung practice, but one of the most interesting ways in which the practice has affected me is in my emotional landscape. Emotions in the recovering addict can be a serious obstacle to the enjoyment of recovery. They can even be the catalyst for a complete relapse. The problem is that we are not used to "feeling feelings," as they say. So when these unrestricted emotions come into play in recovery we are often overwhelmed.

Addressing emotional states with Chi Kung is normally considered an intermediate practice, after one has become proficient in purifying and circulating chi. Dashi Steve and I both agree that emotions are such a serious issue for recovering people that the sooner we gather tools to assist in assimilating those emotions the better. Mostly I have found that many of these less comfortable emotional states tend to locate somewhere in the body. This is in complete alignment with Chi Kung teachings. But, to know it is one thing, to experience it is another.

When emotions would arise, I began to look to the body. I began to see where the emotions were settling in the body. This is easier with strong emotions, like anger, fear, and sadness. My aim in the beginning was to change the emotion, to make it other than it was. My practice of mindfulness has softened this area somewhat. I have found it more useful to allow the emotion to arise, settle, and then dissipate, while maintaining awareness of its location in the body and allowing the energy to flow in this area instead of becoming trapped.

For example, instead of just "getting angry," on one occasion I was able to notice anger arising in my body, as well as the very strong flow of energy that came with it. Immediately when I focused my attention on the flow of energy in my body, I relaxed the reactive tendency in my mind—the habit energy that before would have had me wanting to jump up, slam a door, yell loudly, or act out in any number of physical reactions. Instead, I just sat and felt the energy, in this particular case carrying anger, flowing throughout my body. It was a strong and strange experience. Chi Kung allowed me to notice this very distinctly.

As the energy flowed it increased and increased. My face and ears grew warm as blood was carried there. My heart started to beat strongly and my breath felt constricted. I sat and did nothing except feel and follow the flow. I was quiet and aware, acutely aware of everything in my body. Then when it felt as though I would explode, the energy plateaued; and then it began to slow down. I felt the heat drain away from my ears and face. My heart returned to a normal heart rate and my breathing became fuller and less constricted. I returned to stasis without having to force something and without having to immediately change my experience in a reactive way.

When the energy returned to balance, I calmly and respectfully expressed myself to the person with whom I was engaged. I stated how I felt and why. It wasn't like I did nothing while the anger peaked. In fact, I did a lot. It just wasn't habitual. I observed. I felt. I listened. I experienced fully what anger felt like in my body and then responded from a place of truth, balance, and wisdom. This was new territory for me, and groundbreaking in its implication for transformation in my emotional landscape.

That is not to say that I experienced every angry episode in this way. But the possibility was now evident. I had experienced something different and it was my job to integrate it into my life more often. This is the way we truly change our behavior. I also experienced the same type of transformation with other emotions, such as sadness and anxiety. I have found Chi Kung and mindfulness practice to be very complementary. There is a deeply mindful aspect to Chi Kung practice and an energetic awareness to mindfulness that work extremely well together. Perhaps they are not separate at all. I know that is how they have evolved in my life.

Dashi Steve once had a dream of creating a school that would train Tai Chi Chuan teachers. I never wanted to teach and I told him so. I just wanted to train, learn my forms, and reap the benefits for myself. But he had other ideas. As my experience progressed, he would occasionally trick me into teaching. He would say something like, "I have to talk to this potential student. Can you just do the warm-ups for me?" Of course I said yes. And then one time he just didn't come back after the warm-ups. He just continued to talk and, sensing the importance of what he was doing, I went ahead with the class. At the end a few students thanked me and commented on what a "natural" teacher I was. It basically grew from there. Dashi Steve believes teaching Tai Chi Chuan and Chi Kung is how we keep the arts alive, both in the world and in ourselves. I have been training with him since April of 1997 and have advanced to the level of Black Sash Associate Instructor, which I received in June of 2005.

Our school is called The Lohan School of Shaolin. We have a small Buddhist temple at our school that we call the Lohan Spiritual and Cultural Center. Dashi's dream is to keep the full traditional art of **Shaolin Kung Fu** alive, complete with the Buddhist spirituality included. On November 11, 2009 I was ordained a **Ch'an** Buddhist priest in the Lohan order of Hsu Yun. We have twelve ordained priests in our organization. Seven serve locally with the other five serving in New Mexico, New York, California, and Georgia. We are the living embodiment of Dashi Steven Baugh's dream.

So here I am, twenty-five years later. Once a hopeless dopefiend who couldn't stay out of emergency rooms, I am now a recovering addict and Buddhist priest who teaches Buddhism, Chi Kung, and meditation to recovering addicts. I have found Buddhism to be a very useful philosophy for people in recovery because it emphasizes what each person can do through thought, word, and deed to eliminate suffering. If there is one thing a recovering addict understands it's suffering, and recovery is basically the elimination of that suffering. They fit so well together; particularly if an addict feels daunted by the sometimes overbearing emphasis on a Judeo-Christian conception of God that can pervade twelve-step meetings, in spite of the emphasis on spirituality as opposed to religion.

Buddhism is something people can practice and still recover within the Twelve Steps, while developing and maintaining a different understanding of God. Kevin Griffin addresses this subject thoroughly in his books, *One Breath at a Time* and *A Burning Desire*. If the topic interests you, check out his books and his website at kevingriffin.net. There are also groups around the country that examine the correlations between Buddhism and the Twelve Steps. Many of these, like the one I host in Las Vegas, can be found on the Buddhist Recovery Network at buddhistrecovery.org.

I decided, in response to more than a few requests, to write this book and I've done so with the intent of passing forward to others what I have received and experienced in my life. If you have sought out and found this book, I hope it inspires you to broaden and deepen the base of your recovery through the practice of Chi Kung.

Chi Kung and Its Benefits for Recovery

The Tao

The Chi Kung exercises presented in this book come to us through a traceable Taoist lineage. The question then arises, what is this **Taoism** or the **Tao**?

Tao is the mystery beyond all mysteries, and the doorway to all existence. So great, so profound, that it cannot be grasped by mere rational means.

Taoists believe that it is mankind's inability to see itself as part of a greater whole that lies at the root of all our suffering, confusion, and ignorance.

If human beings could balance themselves within the greater whole, they would lead a simpler life of happiness and understanding. The Tao is harmony. The Tao is balance. The Tao is ever present and elusive. It is the question as well as the answer. The image used by Taoist to represent the harmonious emphasis of their philosophy is the **"Yin-Yang"** symbol.

The Chinese character for Tao shows a person walking on a path, neither male nor female. Each individual can know Tao directly. There is no need for organized religion, orthodoxy, scripture, or social conformity. There is only the need for direct experience. However, few people manage to experience such contact. Modern life presents us with many distractions and numerous potential sources of disharmony. This is reflected in the tension between our careers and our personal lives, our relationships and our families, and between other aspects of our needs and interests. We are often conflicted in our daily goals and priorities. Does this sound familiar? In Chapter Four of *Narcotics Anonymous*, in the preamble to "How It Works," the following question is raised:

"Do we know that our addiction changed us into someone we didn't want to be: dishonest, deceitful, self-willed people, at odds with ourselves and our fellow man?"[4]

Addiction exacerbates the proclivity for disharmony that pervades the way most people live their lives. Taoists understand this and work toward balancing or harmonizing all aspects of life into an integrated, harmonious way of being.

In our modern way of life, the way we think, the way we take care of our bodies, and the philosophy we hold are often disconnected from one another. We are people whose lives are a web of contradictions. The solution lies in finding a way to organize and reconnect all these disparate elements of ourselves.

Furthermore, the Taoists believe that it is only by balancing all of these elements that we are able to "know the Tao." This balance is what leads to a complete way of life that is deeply spiritual. A spiritual life deeply rooted in the body and in life itself. The spirit is not separate from any other aspect of living. This is something that recovering people come to realize—that their lives become spiritual. But we often fail to incorporate our spirituality into our physical being, into our physical experience. In Taoism nothing is overlooked. What you eat, how you exercise, how you treat your body—all of it is as important as how you think and what you believe.

I am not trying to convert anyone to Taoism by any means, but through this philosophy we can see the possibility of harmony and balance enriching our recovery and our lives. Additionally, it is good to know where the exercises I will describe come from and why they have been practiced down through the centuries.

A Brief History of Chi Kung

Chi Kung has a long history in China dating back to China's First Emperor, Qin Shi Huang. Originally, Taoists were trying to achieve immortality through the ingestion of herbs and metallic compounds. Many of these compounds were poisonous, such as mercury and lead, leading to many deaths during this period. Fortunately, at some point Taoists decided that cultivation of vital force or chi was enough to bring longevity, and so they settled for that instead. They started to rely on the cultivation of chi as the road to extending life and performing extraordinary feats.

By the second century CE, Taoists were mimicking the behavior of animals, which are extremely efficient at expending and conserving energy. Cranes, geese, and tigers are exceptional examples of this. Cranes can stand completely still for long periods of time and then explode into very powerful and accurate movement in order to catch fish. Geese are large birds that can fly long distances without stopping while migrating. It takes a great deal of energy to move such a large animal through the air for such an extended period of time. Tigers are superb hunters that can move silently and smoothly through tall grass, stopping and waiting when need be and then moving quickly in a strong dynamic movement designed to surprise prey. When viewed this way, birds and animals can be models for energetic strength and power. The exercises that were practiced to imitate these animal movements were called **"Dao Yin"** (guiding and stretching) exercises, the precursor of Chi Kung.

The Taoists were also wanderers and they began to adopt breathing methods from other cultures. By the Tang dynasty (seventh to the early tenth centuries CE), they had incorporated the **Yogic** practice of **pranayama** into Chi Kung. They also borrowed methods of Buddhist breathing and exercise. **Bodhidharma**, the twenty-eighth patriarch of Zen Buddhism, is believed to have brought many exercises to the **Shaolin temples** in the fifth or sixth centuries. Many of these exercises are still practiced today. Bodhidharma's "Muscle Change & Marrow Washing Classic" is one of the most famous, particularly in Shaolin Kung Fu schools. Bodhidharma is credited with fusing "Ch'an" (the Chinese rendition of the word "Zen") Buddhism with the **"Long Fist Style" of Kung Fu**. Long Fist Style was practiced by mercenaries sent by Emperor Liang Wu Ti to protect the Shaolin temple where Buddhist scripture was being translated from Sanskrit into Chinese. After Bodhidharma's introduction, these traditional monks, along with unconventional soldiers, became the first Warrior monks, and Shaolin became famous for its high level of martial arts and spirituality. In addition, **"Treasure Vase" breathing exercises** traveled to China from the Tibetan **Vajrayana** and **Tantra** traditions.

Lu Dongbin is popularized as one of the **Eight Immortals** in Taoism—a group of legendary beings in Chinese mythology. He is considered a great scholar and the Third Patriarch of the **Quanzhen School (Complete reality school) of Taoism**. He is also the founder of the **Golden Dragon Temple** in China. It is Lu Dongbin and Chong Li who are credited with teaching the **"Golden Elixir" style of internal alchemy**. This is the method that was moving away from the deadly and unsuccessful attempts at achieving immortality that had been practiced previously. Golden Elixir emphasized inner cultivation and spiritual immortality instead. This method concentrated on nourishing the spirit through tranquility and emptiness as well as extensive Chi Kung exercises.

Share Lew was one of the last living survivors of the Golden Dragon Temple and was forced to flee to the United States during China's Cultural Revolution (1966–1976). He resided in San Diego, California, for many years, passing away only recently on July 16, 2012, at the ripe old age of ninety-four. Share Lew personally taught my teacher, Dashi Steven Baugh, Chi Kung and various other practices and rituals of the Quanzhen school of Taoism.

Even though the origins of Chi Kung can be traced back thousands of years, the exercises that we practice today are generally very different from those ancient origins. They are in fact a synthesized product, refined by dedicated masters of Chi Kung intent on developing the best way of cultivating this energy that is so necessary for a healthy, harmonious existence.

The Physical Aspect

We know that addiction affects us mentally, spiritually, and physically. For many of us the physical effects of our addiction are glaringly obvious. Living through active addiction means that we have spent a lot of time abusing our bodies. The deteriorated state of our bodies when we reach recovery—if we reach it—is often a driving force behind seeking recovery to begin with. For others the physical state of the body is accepted with resignation and a sense of foreboding that belies our efforts to stop using. However, once in recovery, the physical aspect is ignored by a large segment of the recovery community. There are many reasons for this, but mostly it's that we are so overjoyed about not having to find ways and means to destroy ourselves on a daily basis that the physical is the least of our concerns. After all, isn't it our desire to "feel good" at all cost that drove our addiction in the first place? It sometimes becomes the driving force in our recovery, too.

The only problem is that feeling good all the time is impossible to achieve and contrary to the laws of nature. The physical, mental, and spiritual aspects are all interrelated. As the saying goes, we are spiritual beings having a human experience. The spiritual and the human aspects are not meant to be experienced separately. Ignoring or neglecting the physical aspect of our recovery disconnects us from our spiritual path. In fact, neglecting ourselves physically often indicates a weakness in our emotional or spiritual condition.

If we had to detoxify from the substances we used to fuel our addiction then we started our recovery up close and personal with the physical aspect. But after that we drop it like a hot potato. It's just not glamorous enough for our stimulus-dependent psyches. And, let's face it, exercising and eating right is hard work. It takes time to learn how to take care of our bodies. It is much easier to take it easy, relax, chill out, and eat foods that have a tendency to taste good and appeal to that pleasure-seeking part of our nature. Inadvertently, we reinforce that tendency toward instant gratification again through eating. Some of these pleasure foods are not very good fuel for our bodies. Many of us go in the other direction, vacillating between indulging and bouts of deprivation through dieting and extreme exercise that often replicates the symptoms of our addiction. We need to take a good hard look at our bodies and the way in which we are treating them. Is the treatment supportive of a person seeking to address all aspects of the disease of addiction? Is it reflective of a person realizing his or her potential to live much longer than previously expected? Are we recognizing the interrelated nature of our lives?

Many of us in recovery reunite with our families and sometimes we create new ones. We become valued assets in other people's lives. Is our physical recovery such that it guarantees we will be around for awhile and be able to share ourselves with our families and friends, or is it based in our self-centered apathetic behavior, driving us closer and closer to an early departure from this plane of existence?

If you are new to recovery you should give yourself a break. This is not meant to make you feel guilty or depressed over yet another area in which you may be falling short. It is simply meant to raise your awareness of an area that has great potential for growth in freedom and vitality—to help you live a life that is healthy and truly worth living. If you have been around for a while, have worked the steps, are overall in a good place in your life and your recovery, and yet recognize something familiar in the idea of having neglected your physical well-being, then perhaps this will provide a call to arms for you—a wake-up call to remind you to make some changes that are supportive of a person in recovery who values life.

Changing the way we relate to our bodies is about changing the relationship we have with our bodies. Currently, it may be healthy or it may be unhealthy and dysfunctional, just like our interpersonal relationships. Bringing awareness to our bodies is a matter of simply paying attention to our physical selves. What are our bodies telling us? Are we depriving ourselves of nutrition in order to "look" a certain way? Are we indulging ourselves wantonly, not caring about the effect it has on our organs and our health? Are we lazy and listless because of the types of "fuel" we are putting in our bodies? Do we lack energy because we create conditions that support low energy? If we look deeply and honestly, our bodies will tell us what we need to know. At that point the decision to act becomes a choice we can no longer deny.

Food

I want to make it clear that getting to the point of being mindful of the physical aspect of recovery has been a long process for me. Like many people, I discovered food when I stopped using drugs. I didn't have to worry so much about weight (I am blessed with a high metabolism), but I did indulge in unhealthy eating habits. I ate anything and everything I wanted, regardless of its nutritional value. I do like vegetables and some healthy foods but I would still gravitate toward the bacon, the burgers, the ribs, etc. It's only recently that I made some changes in this particular area, and I am now mostly vegetarian. A **"flexitarian,"** if you will. I do eat some meat occasionally. The way this change happened for me is interesting.

My partner Leanne and I watched a documentary about the value of replacing animal protein and fats with whole and plant based foods. I was hesitant at first due to my strong emotional attachment to certain foods, as well as some misconceptions I had about "my need for animal protein" given my high energy lifestyle. These misconceptions were dispelled by the documentary. Leanne turned off the TV and declared, "That's it. I'm going to change what I eat!" She is that type of person and I knew with that declaration that she would indeed make it happen. I, on the other hand, cringed inside. I decided I would "give it a try." What did I have to lose? I remember saying the same thing to myself when I walked into my first twelve-step meeting twenty-four years ago.

Another thing that happened is that I began to look at food consumption differently, almost mindfully. Up until that point food had simply been a form of fuel for me, with a heavy layer of pleasure-seeking on top. Often the pleasure-seeking would overshadow the nutritional part. So I started to think of food more as fuel. Since the type of fuel I consume determines how well my body will function and for how long, I should probably be more mindful of the kind of fuel I eat. I started to become aware of the pleasure-seeking or self-soothing nature of my eating habits. I wanted to eat "clean." It made sense. I'm not saying I will never again eat anything unhealthy. What I am saying is that I am very conscious about that choice. It is important to try and relate to the body and its appetite with compassion and acceptance through this awareness process. It is not meant to be another source of guilt for you to deal with.

Leanne and I spent hours compiling recipes for foods that were plant-based and had good nutrition. The reality is that if it doesn't have good flavor I probably won't continue eating it for very long. So far the result is that I feel better physically. I feel lighter and stronger with no lethargy after eating like I used to have. I am a little surprised by how much the attraction to unhealthy foods has dissipated. Once I started looking at it from a different perspective, from a clearer perspective, unhealthy foods became less desirable. The other thing I have been vigilant about is not to judge people who still eat the way I used to, or worse. Nobody likes a know-it-all. I would love for more people to eat healthily, but as we say in my twelve-step program, it is about attraction not promotion. If someone asks, I tell them and try to encourage them. If not, then I don't say anything. Also, in my efforts to live a life of "non-harming" toward all living things, I have noticed a subtle sense of joy about eating things that are not the result of an animal dying. Not completely abstaining, mind you, but well on the way.

So my point, in a nutshell, is that you can change the way you relate to food and its consumption. Is it aligned in a manner consistent with addiction: mindless disregard for health, harmful, and self-centered? Or is it aligned in a manner consistent with recovery: mindful, compassionate, and informed of its effect on the body, mind, and spirit?

Sex

Eating and nutrition are just one way in which our physical well-being is affected in our recovery. Sex is another. Sex is centrally rooted in the pleasure-seeking centers of the brain and it is often an area in which recovering people struggle. For some it is the entire scope and manifestation of their addiction. For others it was just a pleasurable side note during their active drug addiction and is now ripe with potential for abuse and harm since they've put down the substances. The unwholesome patterns of behavior in this area are as varied as the addicts themselves. It runs the gamut from selfish, self-serving patterns of manipulation and gratification to severe forms of abuse, neglect, and exploitation. Along the way the possibility of contracting life-threatening diseases is either ignored or lied about. Some of the deepest wounds we have experienced fall under the umbrella of sex. Being able to heal and practice different behavior in this area is one of the greatest benefits of recovery. We share and examine parts of ourselves we never felt possible before, in our newfound safe, nurturing environment, where there is no fear of reprisal or judgment. It goes without saying that the more delicate aspects of this subject must be addressed with great trust and acceptance.

There are numerous suggestions for healthy behavior as it pertains to sex and relationships. Many suggest that we abstain from relationships altogether for the first year or at least until we have completed Steps Four and Five. Very few people listen to this advice but it has a basis in practicality. How can we expect not to harm or to change for the better when we haven't even identified what needs to be changed? Not surprisingly, things we accepted and did while actively using are not supported in a program of recovery. However, the mind is very powerful and capable of developing elaborate justifications and rationalizations often to support reprehensible behavior. A trusted sponsor is therefore a necessary and invaluable ally in the process of breaking through and confronting areas of denial around sex.

Now that we are learning to live in our bodies and to experience life fully, we can start to express our sexuality in healthy and fulfilling ways. We learn how to be intimate in ways far beyond the physical realm. We learn how to connect in real genuine ways with our sexual partners and experience fulfillment in an area that often left us feeling ashamed and remorseful. Careful choosing and honest sharing with our sponsor, and a support group, are necessary to stay grounded and healthy in our sexual behavior.

Illness and Disability

Another physical aspect of our recovery is illness and disability. Sometimes they are the direct result of our active addiction, including blood-born diseases, immunity problems, organ weakness, nutritional deficiencies, heart disease, and a litany of ailments that are the undeniable effects of repetitious abuse of dangerous substances. Sometimes illness and disability are simply the result of the natural process of aging. It is important to be aware of how guilt and self-pity can affect our health. We can beat ourselves up over the things we did and the effects they had and feel very sorry for ourselves. We can develop a fatalistic attitude, getting trapped in the mindset of "what's the use?" Alternatively, we can truly work a program of recovery and reach some level of acceptance and work from there. Many diseases come with the looming possibility of death in the future, but we can choose to live as if we're dying or we can live each precious moment with joy and gratitude that encourage and enhance not only our own lives but the lives of everyone we come in contact with.

So when confronted with illness and/or disability in recovery we have to reconnect with that same "will to live" that prompted us to seek recovery in the first place. The energy that developed into the miracle of living life without the use of drugs is the same energy that you tap into in order to live life with an illness or disability.

We want to live, or we wouldn't be here at all, so we need to start living in acceptance of whatever life brings. However, to do this skillfully you will need to change some things—once again. You may have to take medications and adjust your level of physical activity for awhile. But you can do this in the spirit of living. You may even choose to adjust your diet to create a more wholesome basis for healing. If we only knew and stayed in awareness of how important healthy, whole foods are to the healing process we would never question this again.

Pain

Many of you reading this book may have issues concerning pain. Perhaps it is the same pain that ultimately fueled your addiction. I want to address this briefly to point out a connection between Chi Kung and some of the new alternative ways of handling chronic pain that are being developed. One alternative treatment modality for chronic pain is **oxygen therapy**. Oxygen therapy is actually a number of related therapies that seek to promote healing and better health by flooding the body with oxygen. Proponents of this therapy explain that pain starts when cells are exposed to decreased levels of oxygen, and that chronic pain is driven by the absence of oxygen. It is a signal from the brain that the cell is not getting enough oxygen, and a warning about a low level of oxygen in the blood—a condition called hypoxia. Nerves are extremely sensitive to cellular oxygen levels. A tiny reduction of it can cause numbness, pain, tingling, and weakness. Therefore, the very best way to optimize your health is to oxygenate all your body's cells, and naturally the best, cheapest, and most effective way to get oxygen therapy is through proper breathing.[5]

Chi Kung is a technique that uses a specific type of breathing to improve health and, in light of this new oxygen therapy model, to diminish pain as well. Of course the ancient Chinese Taoists knew about this a long time ago. In modern usage one of these specific breathing practices has come to be known as **Tan Tien** breathing, which is specifically designed to facilitate the most efficient absorption of oxygen into the body. Tan Tien breathing will be covered thoroughly in Section III.

Aging

And finally I want to address the matter of aging—a natural process in life that many of us never actually believed would occur for us. I personally knew that there was a very high likelihood that I would die before I'd get the chance to bounce my grandkids on my knee and tell them stories about the good old days. I can relate to the sentiment often shared in the rooms of recovery that "If I'd known I was going to live this long I would've planned better."

The fact is, once in recovery, we do age, often for much longer than we could have ever imagined. Many of us get stuck wallowing in regret about all the time we have lost or the damage we have done to our bodies. Getting in touch with our physical bodies is a slow process for many. Trauma, whether from violence, self-abuse, war, or prison, can cause us to experience panic when trying to connect to our bodies.

In recovery we need to learn how to allow ourselves to age. Resistance, as the saying goes, is futile. In fact it is this very resistance that causes suffering; the dissatisfied mind state that tends to pervade our consciousness and thwart our happiness. We will most likely watch many of our friends and acquaintances, in and out of the program, pass away. We may start to imagine our time is shorter than we think. Maybe it is. But nobody knows. All we do know is that we can dramatically increase our longevity by making some simple lifestyle changes.

Aging can be an adventure. It is filled with excitement, wisdom, growth, and joy. The key to aging gracefully is self-acceptance. We balance our attitude somewhere between self-loathing and self-respect, between vanity and humility. With self-acceptance we find ourselves resting in awareness of our place in the world and in the lives of those around us. We become content with all the precious moments and events that we get to experience as a result of the inescapable process of aging.

Throughout the aging process we also inevitably face death. Sometimes we have to face death even before we grow old. Death was "at our doorstep" when we were active in our addiction. In recovery, we have the opportunity to live possibly longer than we expected. We start to cherish and appreciate life, and so the prospect of dying becomes less attractive to us. Yet we see people die. Addicts die due to relapse and addicts die clean. We respond with shock and sadness. When addicts die as a result of using we tend to examine the unskillful actions of that person so that we do not emulate them. When addicts, or friends and relatives who are not addicts, die we experience emotions that we wouldn't want to experience if we had a choice. It is uncomfortable. It is unpleasant, so we look for ways not to feel this pain. Since we are not using anymore and since we have acknowledged that to be an unsuccessful strategy for dealing with pain, we push away in other ways—we avoid, we detach. It feels like the more our heart opens, and the more connected we become, the greater the potential for pain.

The truth is the pain comes anyway, whether we are open and connected or not. We have to be careful on this point that we don't begin to shut down, isolate, and cover up, in our efforts to avoid pain, including fear of our own death. To acknowledge death is to acknowledge life. If we were aware of and connected to the transitory nature of life we would most likely live it with vigor and gratitude. We cannot protect ourselves or run away from the inevitable truth of existence: that we will all die some day. So what is there to do?

Many of us choose to "increase our conscious contact with God as we understand him," thereby gathering a sense of relief and support from a loving presence that has guided us this far. We connect even more to our experience, allowing ourselves to feel whatever is there. We lean into the discomfort and let friends and loved ones support us. And ultimately, we look into the true nature of our experience and embrace it. That may sound difficult and it is. But to do anything else increases suffering, whereas just being with it, and breathing into it, lets us see the impermanence of this and all other experiences. The result of seeing things clearly and acting accordingly is freedom.

Evidence

I realize that most people reading and learning this material will be new to energy-based modalities. We often have a hard time bridging the gap from our everyday perception to believing in something as invisible and mysterious as chi. We want to figure it out and measure it. It is interesting that we don't do this with things like electricity or breathing. We just trust that when we flip a switch the lights will come on, paying little attention to the scientific processes that occur for this to happen. Likewise with the breath, we just trust that we will breathe, with little or no attention to the process that occurs. Chi is much the same. It just happens. However, the gap is there because we don't trust that it will happen or that these exercises will enhance the process.

To help address this I want to bring the following four sources to your attention—books and studies that have been verified by reputable scientific institutions—so that you can be the judge. Regardless of how you decide to think of it in the end, I urge you to practice with an open mind and a willingness to improve your health, so that you may experience the results for yourself.

1) The book, *The Field: The Quest for the Secret Force of the Universe* by Lynne McTaggart describes how chi and paranormal effects are being borne out by quantum physics. McTaggart acknowledges that chi is part of the fourth dimension referred to in quantum physics and she discusses how, in the invisible, subatomic world, energy connects all matter in one holistic whole. Based on this it would seem that Taoists and physicists are in profound agreement about the nature of energy. Science and spiritual masters both agree that everything is linked energetically, and this energy is precisely what we are working with in Chi Kung and Tai Chi Chuan practice.

2) In 1999, D. R. Young (et al.) published an article in the *Journal of the American Geriatrics Society* comparing aerobic and chi exercises. The study was titled, "The Effects of Aeorobic Exercises and Tai Chi on Blood Pressure in Older People: Results of a Randomized Trial," and it showed that the circulation boost for people who spend twenty minutes doing chi exercises is as effective as spending the same twenty minutes doing aerobic exercise. This is good news for diabetics, for instance, who generally have to keep up a fairly rigorous regimen of aerobic exercise to avoid circulation problems endemic to their disease. Oftentimes age, poor health, or injuries prevent them from overcoming these circulation problems with aerobics. Chi Kung and Tai Chi, being much less physically demanding of the participant, are a viable and sustainable form of exercise for diabetics and heart patients, or anyone with circulation affecting diseases. Chi exercises increase the elasticity of blood vessels by increasing the pressure within them. This causes the capillaries to be flooded with blood. Since there is no pressure on the heart to

work harder to boost circulation, there are benefits to chi exercises that are not present in aerobic exercise.

3) Dr. Bruce Lipton, a cellular biologist, conducted research demonstrating that strong, positive intent can exert a powerful healing effect. In his book, *The Biology of Belief: Unleashing the Power of Consciousness, Matter, and Miracles*, Dr. Lipton shows how energetic messages that originate from positive or negative thoughts strongly affect healing processes at the level of the DNA in the cells. The Chi Kung exercises that will be presented in Section III have a strong component of directed mental intention that is used to facilitate healing in practioners.

4) In the August 2010 issue of the *Journal of Alternative and Complementary Medicine* there was an article titled, "Introducing Qigong [an alternative spelling for Chi Kung] Meditation into Residential Addiction Treatment: A Pilot Study Where Gender Makes a Difference." This study, conducted by Kevin W. Chen, Anthony Comerford, Phillip Shinnick, and Douglas M. Ziedonis, introduced Chi Kung meditation to 248 participants for up to four weeks. The results indicated that most clients were amenable to meditation as part of the treatment program, and two thirds chose to participate in daily meditation. The group that chose the meditation protocol as opposed to Stress Management and Relaxation Training (SMART) reported a treatment completion rate of 92 percent versus 78 percent for the SMART participants. And the Chi Kung meditation group reported more reduction in craving than did the SMART group. Female meditation participants reported significantly more reduction in anxiety and withdrawal symptoms than any other group.

The study concluded that Chi Kung meditation appears to contribute positively to addiction treatment outcomes. It also found that meditative therapy was more acceptable or effective for female drug abusers than for males.

欽定屐養齋籍

Exercises: Breathing, Meditation, Chi Kung, and Mindful Movement

Chi Kung is a threefold process. The first is the particular way that you breathe, called Tan Tien breathing. The second is what you are thinking about or the focus of any posture you are doing—this being the mental intention. And the third is the mild physical movements. The physical movements are as soft and relaxed as possible, using the least amount of muscle necessary to perform the movement. The breathing and mental aspects are the most important. It is with those that we move and direct the chi. The physical aspect is mostly used to guide the chi and to train it to go where we want it to. The physical aspect also stretches and stimulates the specific pathways of chi that correspond to the exercise we are working on.

This being said, it is recommended that you modify or omit any posture if there is a chance that performing it would cause you pain or injury. I will detail the modifications for each exercise as they come up. If you need to avoid a particular movement entirely, that is fine. But rather than getting caught up in judgment about what you cannot do, you can use an "envisioning" or visualization process. Envision yourself performing the actual movement, using the same breathing pattern as if you were actually doing it. It is much better to do the exercises this way than to do them physically and cause yourself pain. Pain is counterproductive and actually inhibits the flow of chi. According to **Traditional Chinese Medicine**, pain indicates either a stagnation or a depletion of chi. Envisioning is a very powerful method of doing the exercises and one I use when I'm in a place where it's inconvenient to physically do them, such as at work for instance. Besides, there are studies that show how the brain cannot tell the difference between envisioning a physical routine and actually doing it. The measured brain patterns are identical. Remember, it is the mind and the breath that are the primary movers of chi.

Chi circulates in two ways: in the blood and in the **meridians**. Blood is oxygenated in the lungs, and the oxygen is circulated throughout the body in the bloodstream. When chi circulates in body tissue, it follows specific pathways or meridians. These meridians cannot be found through dissection—they are not tubes, nerves, or even fibers. They are simply patterns of energy flowing through various types of body tissue.

These pathways or circuits can become blocked by illness, stress, poor diet, physical trauma, energetic imbalances in the body, lack of movement, or even improper thinking. Of course addiction, with its physical, mental, and spiritual components, is very effective at causing chi blockages.

The good news is that these blockages can be opened or induced to flow by herbs, massage, or acupuncture. Traditional Chinese Medicine doctors stimulate the meridians, opening those that are blocked and regulating the energy in those that have an excess of chi. Other ways to promote proper energy flow are a healthy diet, proper hygiene, and exercise utilizing the meridian system, such as Chi Kung. Chi Kung translates most simply as "The art of cultivating chi."

Since chi moves through the body along the meridian pathways it is important to keep the body loose during Chi Kung. Even so, the chi tends to slow down when it moves through our joints. This is why we do "lubrication" or warm-up movements to help it flow. These movements provide a full range of motion that strengthens the joints and signals the body to continue producing synovial fluid, which is the natural lubrication in the joints that sometimes dissipates from lack of use, especially as we get older.

Lubrication Exercises

Stand comfortably with your legs a little wider than shoulder distance apart. Extend your arms out in front of you and rotate both wrists simultaneously. Then reverse to the opposite direction. When doing the exercise in two directions, in each direction allow approximately fifteen seconds for each.

Next move to your elbows, trying to keep them stationary as you rotate your forearms inward, then reversing outward.

Next rotate your shoulders and arms forward, then backward, in a windmill motion.

Next rotate your head. Be careful not to grind too vigorously on your cervical vertebrae. A nice long stretch to the sides and front is fine though. Try to relieve the tension that the body loves to hold in the neck.

Next twist your upper body from side to side, loosening up your waist and lower lumbar region. Be careful to move slowly and increase your range of motion as your body allows.

Next rotate your upper body as if there was a large ball in your lower abdomen. Be careful to keep your hips stationary. Rotate in one direction, then the reverse.

Next loosen your hip joints by tracing an imaginary circle with your pelvis. This circle should be about as wide as your stance. Circle in one direction, then the reverse.

Next place your feet together and bend your knees. Bend at your waist so that you can rest your palms on your kneecaps. Press lightly with your hands to help support your kneecaps while they settle into their proper position. Pull your belly button up toward your spine. And don't rest your weight on your knees. When ready, rotate your knees slowly in a circle, drawing imaginary circles with your fingertips. Reverse direction.

Next place your right foot behind you, resting on the toes. Rotate your ankle, pivoting on the toes to get a full range of motion. Reverse direction. Switch to the left foot and repeat.

Now that your joints are nice and loose we will move on to the breath.

Tan Tien Breathing

The way you breathe during Chi Kung is of maximum importance. The type of breathing we will use for these exercises is called "Tan Tien" Breathing. Tan Tien translates as "elixir field" and refers to an area of the body where chi naturally collects and stores. The Chinese often refer to chi as "elixir," something valuable and healing.

Begin by finding a comfortable posture with your feet about shoulder distance apart. Your knees should be relaxed. Your back is straight with your sacrum (lower back pelvis area) tilted back slightly to flatten the lower back. Your head should feel as if suspended by a cord from your crown point (top of the head).

Your chin can be tilted down slightly to straighten the back of the neck. Your tongue gently touches the roof of the mouth (thereby continuously stimulating and balancing all of your body's acupuncture meridians). Your teeth and mouth are closed, but not clenched. You want the entire body to be as soft and relaxed as possible.

Position your thumbs by your navel with your palms flat on your abdomen with the fingers of one hand lying on top of the fingers of the other hand. This should leave a diamond shaped space on your abdomen defined by your hand position. This diamond area about three inches inside the body is the place referred to as the Tan Tien (the elixir field)—more specifically, the "lower" Tan Tien and the only Tan Tien we are interested in at this time (Figure 1).

When you inhale you want to breathe into this area. So your abdomen should inflate or expand slightly as you inhale. When you exhale your abdomen should collapse slightly as the air releases out of your body. This should be in synchronization with the breath. Be careful not to use too much force while breathing. The breath should not make any sound inhaling or exhaling. Moderation is the key. Imagine your lungs filling with air from the bottom up. Be sure to keep your shoulders relaxed during the breathing. Resist the temptation to hunch or raise them in any way. In the beginning there may be very little movement of your abdomen. It takes a little bit of practice, but in no time at all you will be breathing a deep cleansing and invigorating Tan Tien breath.

FIGURE 1

It takes effort for adults to practice this type of breathing, but infants are born breathing this way. If you have a baby you can observe, take notice of the way he or she breathes and then reflect on why it is that we stop breathing this way. It is a healthy way of breathing and should be practiced often. You can do it anywhere. The next time you have idle time, when you are standing in line at the supermarket and losing your patience, waiting to be seen by a doctor, or waiting for a bus, or find yourself in any of the numerous time-wasting activities that we engage in on a daily basis, you can practice Tan Tien breathing. Don't waste time—breathe!

You can skip the hand posture if it makes you self-conscious. It can also be done seated. Just make sure you keep your back relatively erect. This type of breathing increases the amount of oxygen we bring into the lungs and the bloodstream, which is a very good thing. Most people breathe with only 60 percent or less of their lung capacity. It also has a way of calming our state of mind and soothing our nervous system. It's exactly what people tell you to do if you get angry, right? "Sit down, take some deep breaths." There is a reason for this. It works.

Breathing helps relieve tension and anxiety. When we are stressed, nervous, or angry, adrenaline is released and the nervous system locks up. Our breathing becomes shallow and often we briefly hold our breath. This becomes conditioned and habitual over time. Tissue, muscles, ligaments, and tendons become tense and constricted, cutting off oxygen and blood flow in your internal organs. Chi Kung breathing exercises neutralize this effect, calming and relaxing your body as you improve the circulation of fluids around and in your organs.

Tan Tien breathing has also been known to help regulate the function of the heart. It strengthens the liver, spleen, and kidneys, which are **"Yin" organs** that support the heart according to the **Five Element Theory** of Traditional Chinese Medicine.

Now that all your joints are lubricated and you have learned how to breathe properly, we have to prepare the body for chi work by doing the three Chi Awakening exercises. These exercises are designed to signal to your body, mind, and spirit that you are about to do Chi Kung. At the Lohan School of Shaolin, we do these three Chi Awakening exercises before every class.

Chi Awakening Exercises

1. Gathering Chi from Heaven
Stand with your legs a little wider than shoulder width apart, arms hanging loosely at your sides.

Your back should be straight and your head level as if suspended from a cord. Your tongue should rest gently on the roof of your mouth. You should breathe in and out through the nose.

Inhale as your arms move slowly out and up in graceful arcs. It is as if you are reaching up to pull down a cloud (Figure 2). When your hands

FIGURE 2

are almost touching above and in front of your head, you begin to exhale as they descend in front of your body. They are close together now and come to rest gently on your Tan Tien. Your movements should be coordinated with the breath. Repeat the desired number of times. Traditionally, the form is repeated three, five, or eight times. You are replenishing your chi reserves with this posture.

FIGURE 3

2. Gathering Chi from the Earth

Your legs stay in the same position as before. Your tongue is still resting lightly on the roof of your mouth. And you continue to breathe in and out through the nose.

Inhale as you begin to raise your arms up in front of you. Keep them extended, but don't lock out the elbows. Use your mental intention to feel the chi rising up through the soles of your feet, your legs, and settling in your Tan Tien. Your arms are acting much like the handle on a pump. When your arms reach shoulder height, you begin to exhale and lower them (Figure 3). You pull your elbows back slightly toward the sides of your body to round out the movement. It feels like your elbows are leading the movement. When your arms get to your sides begin again. Your breath should be coordinated with your movements, neither jerky nor disconnected.

Repeat this exercise the same number of times you did the first exercise.

3. Combining Chi from Heaven and Earth

Your posture and breathing is the same as in the previous two exercises. This time your palms are facing up with your fingertips almost touching in front of your Tan Tien.

Inhale as your hands rise up in front of your body. When they get to the level of your heart they turn over and face out (Figure 4).

At this point you hold your breath as you press away from your body. When your arms are almost fully extended you start to exhale (Figure 5).

FIGURE 4

FIGURE 5

While exhaling, your hands split apart and move to the sides in slow moving arcs, ending when they are extended out from your sides (Figure 6).

And then slowly lower your hands to your sides as you use your mental intention to continue the circle around your back where you can't reach. You are completing the circle this way. In actuality it is a sphere. This chi sphere completely encapsulates your body. When you are inhaling you should imagine or feel chi entering the crown of your head and up through your feet and legs. Both energies meet in your Tan Tien. A ball of chi in your Tan Tien begins

FIGURE 6

to rotate from the force of combining these two powerful energies in your body.

This is a deceptively simple, yet powerful posture and should be practiced often. It is also an excellent way to clear off your **etheric body**—the part of you that is actually outside of your body. This exercise drastically increases your sensitivity to this energetic or etheric body. Most of us have had experiences with this. Can you recall any times when you knew someone was standing close behind you even though you didn't see or hear them? They were in your energetic field or etheric body. The mind, body, and spirit intrinsically sense these types of things. This causes us to step back if the intrusion is foreign or unfamiliar, and welcoming if we trust or love that person. In modern slang we use phrases like, "You're in my space, man" to refer to this area, close to but outside of our physical body.

Thus far we have lubricated our joints, practiced our Tan Tien Breath, and awakened our chi. It is time to move on to the Eight Section Brocade exercises.

Eight Section Brocade ("Ba Duan Jin")

Form 1. Prop Heaven to Improve the Functions of the Triple Warmer "San Jiao"

This posture is used to reduce stress and tension or any negativity. It also improves circulation and stimulates the **Triple Warmer (San Jiao)**, which regulates the functions of the fluids within the internal organs.

Stand with your feet shoulder width apart and with your feet straight like you are standing on railroad tracks. Your knees are relaxed, your back is straight, your head up like it is suspended by a cord. Your chin is tilted down slightly to straighten the neck. Place your tongue on the roof of your mouth behind your teeth. Your arms are hanging

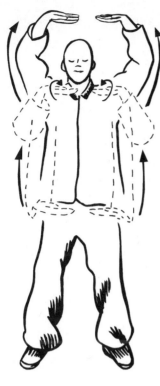

down with your palms facing up, and the fingertips of each hand are pointed toward each other.

Inhale and slowly raise your hands up in front of your body. When your hands get to your shoulders, they turn over and press upward in a "propping" motion (Figure 7).

Exhale through your mouth and let your arms float down to your sides. With each exhale you should imagine any stress or negativity flowing out with the breath. Taking it a little further, you can imagine or possibly feel your body actually become lighter as you relieve yourself of stress and negativity.

FIGURE 7

Repeat three, five, or eight times.

Form 2. Draw the Bow to Shoot the Duck

Very few addicts haven't done some harm to their lungs, so this is an excellent exercise to help get them back in shape. It is estimated that 40 percent of people use less than the full capacity of their lungs and many more are what we would call "shallow breathers." As they age their lungs become weaker and they experience shortness of breath. This in turn leads to ill health, weakness, and depression. Breath awareness is as important to health and longevity as diet or proper rest.

This posture strengthens the lungs and balances chi on both sides of the body. It is also used to extend the connection between heaven and earth through our bodies. This is called the celestial stem or **"Tien Gunn."** Even though the posture stresses movement to the sides, we use our minds to connect the celestial stem straight through our bodies up into the heavens.

FIGURE 8

Stand in a wider stance known as **"Ma Bu"** or horse riding stance. The feet are wider than the shoulders apart, with toes pointing straight ahead. Upper body is straight like a cord is pulling up from your head throughout the posture. Inhale as your right hand/arm draws across the front of your body in front of your abdomen in a scooping motion. At the same time, your left arm extends out from your shoulder parallel to the floor with your index finger pointing upward and your thumb down and out, forming the letter L. Be sure and leave the elbow slightly bent to allow chi to flow through the joint better. Continue to bring the right hand up to meet your left while turning slightly on your waist. Grab an imaginary bow string and draw it across your chest, still inhaling and pull your shoulder back as you expand the lungs fully (Figure 8).

Hold slightly, then exhale through the nose and relax/sink slightly into your posture. Repeat on the opposite side: scooping with your left hand, extending your right arm, and turning slightly to the right. Drawing the imaginary bow string across your chest with the left hand until the left arm is pulled back and you feel a stretch through the chest. The lungs should be full and expanded at this point. Then you release the arms and the air from your lungs as you exhale through your nose and sink slightly into your horse-riding stance. That completes one set. Now repeat as many sets as you like. Usually three, five, or eight sets. As you progress you can begin to add the sacred sound, "SSSSS" on your exhalation. This helps to neutralize sadness and grief, which tend to get stuck in the chest and lungs.

Form 3. Raise Single Arm to Regulate the Functions of Spleen and Stomach

This posture harmonizes the energies of the stomach and the spleen. It also aids digestion by moving energy through the small and large intestine meridians.

Stand with your feet in the shoulder width stance, your back straight, head suspended, and your tongue on the roof of your mouth. Your arms are by your sides. Turn your wrists toward the front of your thighs so that your fingertips point toward each other with your palms facing up in front of your thighs.

Start inhaling (deeply into your Tan Tien) as you slowly raise your hands in front of you maintaining

FIGURE 9

the palm up position. When they rise to the level of your heart they split: your right hand rises up above your head with the palm flat toward the sky, your left hand moves down and next to your left hip with the palm facing down (Figure 9).

Exhale and let the raised arm slowly float down to your side as if on a cloud. Alternate this position by raising the opposite arm with the same breathing pattern. Inhale as you raise the arm and exhale as you lower it. This completes one set. You can repeat as many sets as you wish.

This posture also helps strengthen your connection between heaven and earth. The Taoists believe that the human form is one of the major connection points between these two powerful forces of nature. You are actually becoming a battery of sorts as you absorb energy through the palms of your hands when they are in the extended position. This posture is also closely related to the accumulation and storing of energy in your Tan Tien that in turn contributes to your increased stamina and vitality. After some time you will be able to feel sensations in your palms as your body gets used to absorbing energy through your palms. The emotion of worry tends to affect the stomach, so we can use a sacred sound to help neutralize it. There are two types of worry. Situational worries like our bills, our job, or any other daily-life type things. And then there are worries of a compassionate nature, like for our loved ones. So there are two sounds that you use. For the first, the situational worries, the sound is "SHU." The sound for compassionate worries is "HAW." But "Haw" is not so much a verbal sound as an internal vibration, so it sounds like you are trying to clear your throat.

Form 4. Looking Back to Alleviate the Five Strains and Seven Impairments

The **"Five Strains"** are activities that cause strain on the five Yin organs: the heart, spleen, lungs, kidneys, and liver. They are excessive standing, walking, sitting, lying down, and prolonged use of the eyes.

Most of these are related to occupational strains, and prolonged use of the eyes can be due to television, computer work, or video games, all of which are prevalent in our modern lifestyles.

The **"Seven Impairments"** affect the constitution of the body: like overeating, fury, cold weather, sorrow, anxiety, laziness (lack of natural early morning energy), and extreme changes in temperature. In addition, this form helps neutralize the effects experienced from great physical or emotional shock. Things like car accidents, violence against your person, or the detoxification process from drug abuse.

Stand with your feet shoulder width apart, knees relaxed, back straight, head suspended, and your tongue placed gently on the roof of your mouth. Your hands are placed on your lower abdomen with your thumbs touching at your navel and your right fingers covering your left fingers (the same as when practicing Tan Tien breathing).

FIGURE 10

As you inhale, your arms open gently as you pull your shoulder blades together and twist your arms so your little fingers are turned up and out. At the same time your head turns evenly to the right, just to a point of comfort, and then your eyes look over your right shoulder (Figure 10).

This all occurs during a long measured inhale. Then after you finish the inhale, your head turns to face the front while your arms come forward and gather chi as you exhale. Ending with your palms settled on your Tan Tien as when you began. On the next inhale your arms open gently as you pull your shoulder blades together with your arms splayed back. This time your head turns to the left. This is followed by an exhale while turning your head to face forward with your hands resting on your Tan Tien. This completes one set. You repeat these movements alternating looking back and forth from right to left. One controlled breath for each side. You can repeat three, five, or eight sets depending on the time allotted for the exercise. This particular exercise is great for people who do a lot of computer work. It helps neutralize the foggy effect of prolonged concentration with the eyes. You are also replenishing your energy stores through this posture.

Form 5. Shake the Head and Twist the Trunk to Extinguish Fire in the Heart
Excess "fire" or heat in the center of the chest, or heart area, is the result of a number of things. Some of the more prominent being lack of sleep, holding in anger or frustration, improper diet (meaning too much food or unhealthy foods), and use of intoxicants, particularly alcohol. This posture works by literally massaging your internal organs with your movement. Our organs typically don't get a lot of massage, so this is an excellent exercise to help keep them supple and flexible, especially as we get older. Many elderly people have stiff, or even brittle, organs and arteries that are prone to disease and failure as a result. The hope is that if we massage them regularly with this Chi Kung exercise we can avoid those effects.

This exercise is performed in the horse stance or Ma Bu as we did in the Drawing the Bow posture. Of course if this deep stance is too difficult, you don't have to place your feet quite so wide. It starts with a yoga-like stretch that you can also omit if it is too difficult. But it is very good for stretching and limbering the lower lumbar region of the spine. From the horse stance you place your hands on your legs above your knees with your elbows out supporting your waist and back.

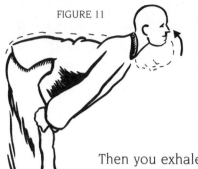

FIGURE 11

You start with your back flat like a table, and then you inhale and sink as you tilt your pelvis/sacrum upward and lift your head and neck up toward the sky—in effect making your back concave (Figure 11).

Then you exhale and bow your back upward like a cat with your head and neck down (Figure 12).

You finish with an exhale as you rise up slowly from the cat posture, one vertebra at a time, until your upper body is vertical. At this point you simply breathe deep Tan Tien breaths as you flex and stretch your torso, chest, and abdomen regions while keeping your hips relatively stationary. Rotate your upper body as you open and close your ribs on the sides in a motion called **"Yin-Yang Ribs"** (Figure 13).

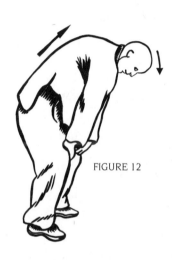

FIGURE 12

FIGURE 13

First, move in one direction for five or eight rotations, then in the opposite direction. Use your mental intention to picture all your internal organs getting a nice gentle massage. There is no coordination between the breathing and the movement, just be sure you breathe. Be conscious of not holding your breath, which seems to be a common tendency. You can also place your hands on your torso to accentuate the motions of your torso. Because of all the flexing on your digestive system, you may experience side effects, such as burping or expelling wind (flatulence). If either of these occur you can smile, because it means you are doing the exercise properly. As uncomfortable as it may be for people around you, it is very good for you. You are releasing gases that impede the digestion process. In fact, in many cultures burping loudly after a hearty meal is considered the ultimate compliment!

Form 6. Touch the Toes to Strengthen the Kidneys and Reinforce the Loins

This exercise increases flexibility of the waist and legs and helps prevent all diseases. It stimulates the meridians of the kidneys and their corresponding organs like the bladder, the gall bladder, the spleen, and the pancreas. There is a specific bladder meridian that runs from the side of the little toe, along the side of the foot, up the Achilles tendon, up the back of the calf, knee, thigh, buttocks, all the way to the kidneys. It actually runs further but that is as far as we will stimulate it with our fingers.

There is bending in this exercise so those with lower back problems can modify the posture by bending their knees while bending over, by widening their stance, or by not bending at all. Remember the physical movements are the least important as far as chi is concerned. They are designed to help train the chi to move along the specific meridians that are being stimulated by the posture and also to get a little bit of stretching into the muscles and tendons. If you do the non-bending method,

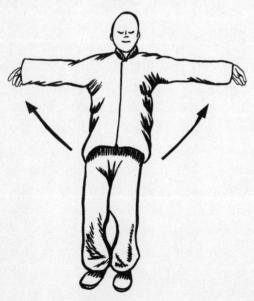

FIGURE 14

simply envision yourself performing the movement as if you were actually doing it. Picture yourself bending and your fingers massaging the bladder meridian running up your leg until you reach your hands and finish up with actual touching.

Stand with your feet in the shoulder width stance as before with your knees unlocked, your back straight, head suspended, and tongue on the roof of the mouth. Inhale as your hands move out from your sides and up to shoulder level with your palms facing down (Figure 14).

Turn your hands slightly and hold your breath as you move your arms toward the front, keeping them extended with the

FIGURE 15

palms facing each other. Imagine chi concentrating in your kidneys at the same time (Figure 15).

FIGURE 16

Now exhale through your mouth as you bend over slowly, folding from the hips, as your arms hang down touching your toes (Figure 16).

While you are hanging there, inhale slowly and circle the fingers of each hand outward.

Now exhale as you slowly run your fingers from the little toes, along the sides of your feet, then up the back of your legs to your kidneys. When you reach your kidneys let your hands rest there, supporting as you arch your back slightly and point your sternum toward the sky with your head tilted back so you are gazing up (Figure 17).

Try to time your exhale so that you don't run out of breath before the movement is completed. Repeat this exercise three, five, or eight times.

Form 7. Punching with Angry Eyes

This posture is most people's favorite, especially addicts. We tend to have a really intimate relationship with the very powerful, negative emotion of anger. Anger is extremely debilitating to all aspects of the human form, and most of us deal with it inappropriately. Anger is expressed through three major outlets: Our eyes—we look at someone in anger or with an angry expression; our

FIGURE 17

mouth—we verbalize our anger, usually at the wrong time to the wrong people in the wrong way, alienating our loved ones and losing jobs and friends because we just had to say what we said in anger; and thirdly through our hands—we hit people and break things, usually glass or expensive personal items. All of these are inappropriate expressions of anger. We didn't come into recovery to experience the kinds of consequences we get when we react this way, so we had better find another way of handling it.

FIGURE 18

The problem with anger or rage is that sitting still and taking ten deep breaths or other such traditional remedies doesn't always cut it. The body, when filled with all that adrenaline, has a need to express itself physically, resulting in holes in your walls and assault and battery charges. In addition, when people become angry or highly focused, they hold their breath. Lack of oxygen to the brain taxes the nervous system, further adding to tension and stress. This exercise is something you can add to your "toolbox" now, to help you through those situations.

Stand with your feet wide in the horse-riding stance. Your fists are soft, not clenched, leaving space in the center. Your thumbs rest lightly on the side of your index finger like you are holding a joystick (Figure 18).

When you punch you do so with the fist held vertical, with a minimum of muscle tension. Your eyes open very wide on the exhale. You will simultaneously exhale through your mouth loudly, punch your fist, and open your eyes wide (Figures 19, 20).

As you inhale and draw your fist back, be sure and relax your eyes. The eyes are the key to the exercise so be sure and open them wide on the exhale and then relax them on the inhale. As you exhale, you visualize beams of light flowing out of your eyes, your fists, and your

FIGURE 19   FIGURE 20

mouth. Any anger you have is expelled from the liver and out of the body on these beams of light. Remember, resentments are subtle forms of anger. The pattern that you punch is: the right side, the left side, right forward, and left forward. You perform three or five sets slowly then three or five sets more quickly with more feeling.

As you progress you can add the sound "SHHHH" to your exhale to help expel anger and to invigorate the liver where, according to Chinese medicine, anger accumulates in the body.

Form 8. Jolt the Body to Shake Away Illness

In general, this exercise helps the body withstand the disharmonious influences of nature and the cosmos. Many illnesses are the result of, or become exacerbated by, stress and emotional weakness. This exercise helps to neutralize these forces and also to bolster or strengthen the immune system by stimulating and "jolting" the lymphatic system itself. The lymphatic system is a major part of the circulatory system that helps the body remove impurities from the blood and tissue. The "negative effects of the cosmos" aspect refers primarily to anyone wishing ill will on you. This causes negative energy to be directed at you. Often, because of social conditioning and the basic inclination for people to want to group together, we inadvertently absorb less than pure energy from others. This posture is helpful in "shaking" off this type of energy, so it is very helpful for massage therapists, reiki healers, psychotherapists, or anyone else working in a healing profession.

Everyone has had experiences absorbing this type of energy. Who among us has not used the expression "He is bumming me out" or "She is so depressing, she is affecting everybody in the office, the house, the kitchen," or any other place where people congregate. The only explanation for negative or depressing people being able to affect others this way is energy. It has to be, because the effects are very noticeable and real, even though the people in question are not touching you or even talking to you.

FIGURE 21   FIGURE 22   FIGURE 23

Stand with your feet shoulder distance apart, your back straight, head suspended as if by a cord, and tongue on the roof of your mouth. You rise up on the balls of your feet as you inhale. Simultaneously, your arms rise from your sides to a position about shoulder height (Figure 21).

Then you exhale and jolt onto your heels as you fling your arms downward in a movement intended to fling something off of them (Figure 22).

It is very important to keep your knees bent as you jolt to diffuse the shock on your spine and neck (Figure 23).

You perform the jolt numerous times, preferably thirty-six, but eight, eighteen, or twenty-four is fine. Normally you inhale up, exhale down, inhale up, and exhale down, in rhythm with your breath. If you find this too strenuous, or you end up hyperventilating, you can take an extra breath at the bottom after you have exhaled to slow down the pace a bit. Also, if you have back, neck, or knee limitations that make it painful for you to jolt in this way you can modify the

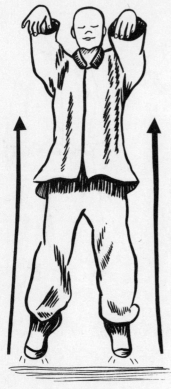

FIGURE 24

posture. Simply use a version I like to call "Springing Legs." You keep your feet flat on the floor and rise up in your stance, then jolt down by bending your knees into the movement so that you replicate a shock-absorber on a car. When your body gets stronger you can switch to the more vigorous method. Honor your body with gentleness and patience. Conversely, if you are young and vigorous you can jump up at the top of the inhale. Again, making sure to land on bent legs to diffuse the shock (Figure 24).

It is always good to take time at the end of Chi Kung practice to seal the energy in some manner. My favorite sealing exercise is "The Cocoon."

Sealing Meditation—The Cocoon

The Cocoon is an ancient Taoist meditation exercise designed to seal chi inside the body. I have taken liberties and expanded on this with some changes. The version that I present here is the one I use and the one I have received the most positive feedback on.

Stand with your feet shoulder width apart, with your feet straight as if standing on railroad tracks. Unlock your knees and straighten your back. Imagine your head is suspended by a cord. Tuck

FIGURE 25

your chin slightly to straighten the back of the neck. Hold your right arm across your chest with your right palm facing your left shoulder, but not touching. Hold your left arm across your stomach with your left palm facing your right hip, but not touching (Figure 25).

Your arms should be in a self-hugging posture. This helps to accentuate the wrapping or cocoon-like effect you are trying to achieve. If, during the meditation, your arms feel too heavy or holding them becomes too much of a distraction, simply lower them to your sides into the **Wu Chi** posture (as described on page 81) and continue from there. It does help with the visualization to at least start from the hugging posture.

Close your eyes and begin your deep Tan Tien breathing as described on pages 58–60. Gradually slow down and lengthen your breath into a nice calming pattern. Now envision a cocoon wrapping around you, sealing the chi inside. The chi is unable to escape from the cocoon. See the chi bouncing between the inside of the cocoon and the surface of your body, like tiny atoms. As the chi bounces back and forth, some of it absorbs back into your skin making your skin more resilient, more impervious to anything negative that would seek to harm you on an energetic or spiritual level. Your skin turns into a shield of protection for your body, which essentially it is.

Now envision the chi going beneath your skin into your muscles and tendons. It bounces around inside them making your muscles and tendons stronger, more able to do the work for which they were intended.

Now envision the chi going into your organs, bouncing around inside them. Envision the chi healing any organs that are sick or damaged and making the healthy ones even stronger.

Now envision the chi going into your bones, your skeletal system. Envision the chi bouncing around inside them, making your bones denser and stronger, better able to support your body. Then envision the chi going into your marrow, an integral part of your immune system. This process invigorates and strengthens your marrow so that you can better fight off disease and infection. You can take it deeper if you like and envision your marrow glowing from inside your bones like a fluorescent light bulb. This is called "marrow washing."

Now we take the meditation to the next level and envision your skin disappearing so that the only thing standing inside your cocoon is your muscles, tendons, organs, and skeleton.

Next envision your muscles and tendons disappearing so that only your organs and skeleton are left standing in your cocoon. Just like an anatomy model.

Next your organs disappear so that the only thing standing inside your cocoon is your skeleton.

Finally your skeleton disappears. So that the only thing left standing in your cocoon, the only thing that could be left, is the essence of your being, your chi. It is sitting inside your cocoon like a luminous egg. It is glowing from the inside out like a fluorescent light bulb.

At this point you can take any spiritual symbol, from any type of spirituality you practice, and place it inside the egg. It can even be your twelve-step symbol. Now you are incorporating your spirituality into the essence of your being on a deeper level. You can add as many symbols to your egg as you like at any time, as your spirituality evolves.

Now envision your body rematerializing around your egg and all the light and energy of the egg extending into all aspects of your being. Your bones, organs, muscles, tendons, and skin are all glowing with the fresh, clean revitalized chi that you have cultivated. Even the space a few inches out from your body is glowing with a white light. Open your eyes when you are ready.

Wu Chi Meditation

Stand with your feet shoulder width apart, knees unlocked, back straight, head up as if suspended by a cord from the crown, chin tucked, and tongue touching the roof of your mouth. The backs of your hands face forward at your sides. Gently pull your arms toward the ground and then slightly out from the body, as if holding tennis balls in your armpits.

FIGURE 26

Be careful not to hunch or lift your shoulders, leave them relaxed. This posture allows for better chi flow along the heart meridians, which run through the armpit area (Figure 26).

You can close your eyes again, if you like, and feel your body and mind sink into a deep sense of relaxation and calm. Your breath slows down and you stand as if tree roots are growing out from your legs and feet deep into the earth. Your upper body remains very relaxed and supple like a willow tree. Now you bring awareness to what is occurring in this place at this particular time.

If you are outdoors, it might be sunshine and the feel of its warmth on your skin, or a slight breeze and the feeling it has as it moves over your body. You might notice different sounds. Maybe a bird singing, a motor humming, leaves rustling, voices, an aircraft, or any number of sounds occurring in your direct awareness. If you are indoors, it might be the ambient temperature of the air on your skin, or the feeling of your clothing draped on your body. The sounds you notice may be of voices of people in proximity to where you stand, an air conditioner or heater motor, a clock ticking, a faucet dripping, a fountain gurgling, whatever is present in your direct experience in the present moment.

Upon noticing them you hold no judgment of them or yourself. You create no stories around them either. You simply let them wash through you as if you were a lace curtain hanging in front of an open window. You are transparent, almost floating. The sounds pass through you as if you weren't there, like the wind. If you prefer, you can picture the sounds washing around you, as if you were a rock in a stream.

Meditate like this as long as you want as often as you can. This is excellent practice. It can be especially helpful in training you to calm yourself. It is vital that any recovering addict find new and healthy ways to self-calm. This is an important skill that will help you better manage any urges you experience to reach for that old familiar substance or behavior.

In addition, this meditation can be very helpful for training yourself for those inopportune times when you have to be around people with "less than healthy" energy. When you notice depressing or negative energy coming your way from someone, you simply acknowledge it and let it pass through you or around you. You don't have to unconsciously absorb this type of energy once you gain an awareness of it and understand how it works. Just like our addiction, until we gain awareness and take responsibility for it, we are powerless to do anything about it.

Again, this is an especially helpful practice for anyone in the healing professions, such as massage therapists, reiki healers, shiatsu practitioners, nurses, doctors, or even counselors. These types of professionals very often accumulate a lot of "energetic baggage" from their work. Often they end up suffering from depression, weakened immune systems, fatigue, and other ailments. According to the laws of science this makes sense. Science states that energy cannot be created or destroyed; it can only be changed or transferred from one place to another. So when healers work on a client, if they do their job right, the "stuff" they are removing from the patient has to go somewhere. The closest possible conduit is often the healers themselves. A healer, being a conduit, is supposed to guide this "less wholesome chi" into the earth where it can be filtered or returned to the source. But during the process, some of it can get stuck in the healer, causing problems. It is very important for anyone who does this type of work to dedicate specific and regular attention to taking care of him- or herself, physically, mentally, and spiritually.

As it relates to learning how to do Chi Kung, above all, practice! These excercises are meant to be practiced regularly. Once a week is good, a few times a week is better. Every day or twice a day is best.

Remember that the more often you do the exercises, the better and more sustained the results will be. And if you claim to be too busy then you need it even more. Keep in mind that the Chinese symbol for being "busy" translates as "heart-killing." It is interesting to me that it has taken the Western world thousands of years to recognize and document the damaging effects of stress and being too busy on our bodies when the Chinese were aware of it as early as when their language first came into being.

Standing Meditation Exercises

In Tai Chi circles there is a commonly held belief that one cannot progress in Tai Chi Chuan or Chi Kung without practicing stillness. In Tai Chi Chuan it is the stillness in the movement that brings out the grace and the power of this beautiful art. But that is for another book. Chi Kung practice, too, has much to gain from standing meditation or stillness.

The following two standing meditation exercises come from my practice in Yang and Chen style Tai Chi Chuan.

1. Yang Style Standing Meditation

With your feet placed about shoulder distance apart, you step out in front with one foot so that just the toe is barely touching the ground. It should be relatively weightless. Your rear supporting leg can be fully extended or locked for support. Your back is straight and your head held as if suspended from a cord. Your tongue should rest lightly on the roof of your mouth. Your arms curve around to form a circle in front of your face. Your palms face your head with your fingertips open, relaxed, and almost touching. Your shoulders should be relaxed and your elbows loose, soft, and hanging slightly (Figure 27).

FIGURE 27

Your gaze is open. You notice your hands, but also everything in your field of vision. Once you are comfortable in your posture, just breathe. You can stand this way as long as you want, just breathing. A few minutes to start is fine. Then gracefully and mindfully switch legs.

Eventually you will want to work up to longer periods of time in this posture. The longer you manage to stay in this position (ten minutes, thirty minutes, even for an hour or more), the more you will notice a great openness or emptiness to your forms when you practice, as well as gracefulness and power that wasn't previously present.

2. Chen Style Standing Meditation

Stand with your feet in the Ma Bu or horse-riding stance. That is twice shoulder width apart with your toes pointing straight as if standing on railroad tracks. Your inner thigh and groin area is rounded as if you were sitting on a horse.

Your arms extend up and are rounded like you are holding up the world. Your shoulders should be relaxed with your palms facing toward each other out to the sides from your head (Figure 28).

Your back should be straight and your head level facing forward. Your tongue should touch the roof of your mouth. This is called the "Heaven" posture. You are absorbing energy from heaven. You envision yourself as a tree, alive and vibrant, reaching up

FIGURE 28

and extending down, rooted in the earth. You can envision fruit developing on your branches. When the fruit is at full complete maturity, you absorb it back into your arms or branches, down into your body and let it collect in a basket resting in your Tan Tien.

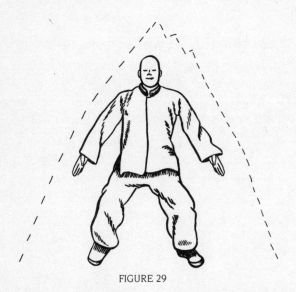

Now you switch to the "Earth" posture. You keep your legs in the same position letting your arms turn over and down. They are out from your body at an approximately forty-five degree angle. Your palms face your body and are loose and open (Figure 29).

FIGURE 29

Envision yourself as a mountain. The mountain is one of the strongest symbols of earth energy. You are still and solid. You are rooted and connected, with roots extending down from your fingers as well as your feet. You are still, yet recognizing and connecting with the movement within the stillness. Just like a mountain.

Finally you switch to the "Mankind" posture. Again your feet stay in the same position and only your arms move. If you are a man, you place the back of your left hand on your **"Ming Men"** point on your spine. If you are a woman you place the back of your right hand there. The Ming Men point is located directly behind your belly button, on your spine. Your right hand (or your left hand for women) curves around gently and rests open and rounded in front of your Tan Tien. Your palm should be facing your Tan Tien (Figure 30).

FIGURE 30

In this posture you envision the energy of heaven flowing into the top of your head. At the same time the energy of earth is flowing into you, up your legs from the soles of your feet. These energies meet in your Tan Tien and form a sphere that begins to rotate or spin with the power of these two strong forces in nature. The human being is the main connection point between heaven and earth and this is expressed in this posture.

If you practice these meditation forms regularly and for increasingly longer periods of time, you will develop great power and a strong sense of connection and harmony.

Mindfulness

I have personally spent a lot of time practicing and teaching mindfulness as both a meditative practice and as a way of being in the world. Mindfulness has transformed my life. It has added a dimension to my existence that is hard to put into words.

Mindfulness is often described as "Paying attention in a deliberate way, without judgment, to the present moment experience." It is non-judging, receptive awareness. This is the opposite of what we do in active addiction. Although the actions in active addiction have a concentrated focus, the entire objective of active addiction is to not experience the present moment. To deny that which is unpleasant and to grasp for that which is pleasant is how addicts live. And there is usually a whole lot of judging going on, of picking and choosing what we do and don't want to experience. A general feeling of never being satisfied is common in active addiction. This can carry over into recovery as well. Mindfulness changes all of that. When mindfulness is strong enough to create some space between stimulus and response, then automatic reactive behavior is weakened, giving us a chance to make wiser choices. Still, there will always be times when it is difficult to break a conditioned response without support of like-minded people. Mindfulness can be an excellent tool for noticing and then modifying our behavior within the context of the supportive and nurturing environments of twelve-step fellowships.

Mindfulness is most often associated with meditation and that is the method by which it is most frequently cultivated. The stillness and quiet usually practiced during meditation is very conducive to being able to train the mind and be mindful—to pay attention to what is really happening in the present moment. To be attentive to our experience in the present moment without conceptualizing, without the stories our thoughts tell us, without the identification, without the judging—that is mindfulness. Unfortunately, most of the time we react and we judge whether we like or dislike what is happening in our experience. Or we compare our experience to our expectations and become harsh and critical of ourselves or others.

Mindfulness reveals the truth of the way things are in life and in our minds. In this respect, it could be said that it is the foundation of all spiritual practice. "The act of paying attention changes how we interpret what is happening to us, and with this insight we become less driven by impulse, reactivity, habit, addiction, or self-will."[6] Can you think of an ability more valuable in recovery than this? In fact, much of the work we do in the Twelve Steps is about getting to this same place. We look closely at our actions, our motivations, our inclinations, and try "to do the right thing," to not react in old, unskillful habitual patterns. We become sensitive to impulsive reactions that create discord and harm, and actions driven by our self-centered desire to fix ourselves from the outside. Mindfulness as a specific method of meditation trains the mind to incline in the direction of wholesome recovery and a non-harming stance in life. "Mindfulness puts us in a position to choose our destiny."[7]

Mindfulness is also being used nowadays as a strategy for reducing stress. Stress is pervasive in our society, where multi-tasking, greed, and one-upmanship are valued traits. Some people maintain that addiction is, at its root, a failed attempt at relieving the stresses of life and life's circumstances. Regardless of the biological and hereditary component, we suffer, or are unsatisfied, with life as we live it. Using substances and certain behaviors to relieve this stress seems like a viable option at first. The only problem is that, for addicts, a biological component kicks in. We come to realize the short-term effectiveness of our strategy, and so we repeat it over and over again until the strategy—the mechanism of our addiction—is no longer relieving our stress, but creating more. So-called "normies," or non-addicts, are somehow able to recognize the flaw in this type of strategy and bring it under control. Addicts, however, generally miss this step. Consequently, we get stuck in a seemingly endless cycle of destruction and despair. Only a drastic awakening of our spirit and our consciousness is able to interrupt this vicious cycle. And maintaining this break in the addictive cycle is what we call recovery.

Awareness of our motivations, of our intentions and our actions is what enables us to sidestep our past conditioning and habits and create new lives for ourselves based on wholesomeness and generosity. Mindfulness by itself is not a cure-all for the complicated and challenging problem of addiction. But it is very good at bringing our issues to the surface and for investigating their true nature. Then we have to approach them with some type of healing process, like the Twelve Steps, therapy, or both. Mindfulness is not really about fixing anything per se. Mindfulness is about seeing things as they are and then being in acceptance of them, even if they are unpleasant or painful. "The practice of mindful awareness is radical self-acceptance, where emotional states are evaluated according to whether they increase or decrease our potential for suffering. For instance: If an emotion, such as hatred, arises that we judge to be destructive, we simply recognize it as such. Then we neither express it through violent thoughts, words, or deeds, nor do we suppress it because we consider it unsuitable to a spiritual way of being. We just see it for what it is: a transient emotional state. And we mindfully observe it as it arises, abides for awhile, then passes away."[8] It is extremely valuable for addicts to view their emotional entanglements in this manner, because emotions and feelings are frequently what get in our way—often triggering reactive tendencies that can end in relapse. The problem is that we have very little experience with this type of awareness, what we call "mindful awareness."

"The practice of mindful awareness can be the first step in the direction toward inner freedom."[9] Very early on in recovery we come to the stark realization that freedom from addiction really is an "inside job." The twelve-step programs as they exist have numerous references to the value of contemplative and reflective practices, but no one shows us how to "pay attention." It's kind of like what we do to children who have problems in school. The teachers— and I remember this quite well—usually say, "Pay attention," "You need to pay attention" or "Why don't you just pay attention?" And when the mind rebels and doesn't cooperate with the teacher's admonishments, we form the conclusion that we are flawed, that "something is wrong with us." We are rarely given proper instruction on how to train the mind to pay attention. There is some work in elementary schools going on right now through the Center for Mindfulness that is achieving remarkable results by teaching children how to practice mindfulness.[10] Imagine that!

There are numerous methods for establishing a practice of mindfulness, but almost all can be traced back to a form of meditation in the Buddhist tradition aimed at cultivating and refining our capacity to pay attention. In Buddhism this is called **"Vipassana"** (**Pali**) or "Seeing things clearly." It is sometimes referred to as "Insight Meditation" here in the West. And this particular method of meditation is exactly what Shakyamuni Buddha practiced in order to achieve full, complete enlightenment or freedom from all aspects of suffering and delusion in the world.

Jon Kabat-Zinn, a biologist and meditator, decided to bring the practice of mindfulness out of the monasteries and Buddhist retreat centers into mainstream America to help the average person relieve stress. He started from very humble beginnings over thirty years ago at the University of Massachusetts Medical School, in a room in the basement. He was able to grow interest in this method of stress reduction by extracting the process of meditation from its Buddhist context and supporting his results with solid scientific evidence. What emerged was a program he called "Mindfulness-Based Stress Reduction" (MBSR), which is now taught and practiced on every continent except Antarctica. He standardized the process and the training to maintain consistency essential to the integrity of his program and the supportive scientific studies. It is an experiential program spanning eight weeks in which participants meet with a trained facilitator for two hours weekly and then complete six days of practice and homework in-between classes. There is also a modality called "Mindfulness-Based Cognitive Therapy," which is taught to therapists as a form of treatment for persistent emotional and psychological dysfunctions. And most recently a related program specific to addiction has emerged called "Mindfulness-Based Relapse Prevention." There are numerous resources available online and in our communities that can help us gain momentum and support as we start to incorporate mindfulness practice into our lives.

Usually mindfulness practice is about being still and bringing attention to bear on our experience while sitting upright. Another method, called "Body Scan," involves lying down where participants are led through a guided meditation that explores the physical sensations as they occur in the body, in the present moment. No matter what the initial teaching posture that is used, they all aim toward a way of being that enables participants to practice mindfulness while walking, eating, sitting, lying down, washing the dishes, playing with our children, working, making love, etc. Virtually any activity in the human sphere of experience can be enhanced by the practice of mindfulness.

A typical mindfulness meditation may sound something like the following example. You can read this slowly and calmly into a recording device to play back while you practice the method or you can have someone else read it to you. You can also access one of the wonderful online resources on mindfulness or buy a mindfulness guided meditation CD. The length will vary, generally anywhere from ten minutes to an hour. It is suggested that you start out with shorter periods and gradually increase the time you practice. In a very short time, if practiced daily, you won't need the guided reference anymore and will be able to guide yourself. However, be sure that you are sufficiently comfortable with the technique so that you don't drift off into day-dreaming or some other, less attentive mind state. Keep in mind that this is not about achieving any sort of altered, blissful, calm, or relaxed state of mind. Rather, it is about cultivating a deeply embodied experience of wakefulness or awareness. Through its cultivation, you may indeed experience very peaceful, relaxed, or calm states, but they are not the direct focus or aim of the practice.

(The ellipses—". . ."—denote pauses of a few beats. Feel free to adapt these pauses to whatever suits your time requirements.)

1. Sitting Meditation

Taking a few moments to shift into a sitting meditation posture. Whether sitting on a meditation cushion, a meditation bench, or a chair, the effort is to sit in a dignified upright posture, wakeful yet at ease. Sitting upright enables energy to flow more easily up the spine, allows the lungs to breathe more easily, and is actually better suited to maintaining stillness over time. We make an effort to remain relatively still throughout the meditation session, because stillness in the body supports the stillness in the mind that we are cultivating. Be careful not to confuse stillness in the mind with peacefulness or calm, at least not yet. The stillness we are interested in is a stability in the midst of whatever is present. That experience may be pleasant or it may be unpleasant—we stay still regardless. However, if you absolutely need to move for whatever reason, by all means do so. But pay attention to that process as well.

Sitting with your back upright and stable, yet at ease, resting your hands on your lap. And gently closing the eyes, if that is comfortable for you.

We begin by letting the attention drop down into the body, noticing all the raw physical sensations present in the body. Notice the sense of weight . . . of pressure where the body touches the cushion or chair, maybe a sense of contact where the hands are resting on the lap, or perhaps some muscle contraction as the muscles work to keep the body upright in the posture. And right there in the center of the physical sensations of the body is the breath—air effortlessly entering the body all by itself, in the present moment. We breathe in the present moment, we breathe now. The breath is a convenient anchor to the present moment, the only place where we are alive. Everything else has happened already or hasn't happened yet. Still we spend so much of our time in the past or the future.

Allowing the breath to anchor you to the present moment and to life itself. It is useful to choose a point where it is easiest to notice the breath. For some it is the nostrils, for others it is the lower abdomen.

Consciously noticing the physical sensation of breathing in and breathing out without trying to control or manipulate the breath in any way. Just letting the body breathe itself. This is where we will rest, and when the mind goes somewhere else, which it inevitably will, we notice that briefly, lightly, nonjudgmentally, and then softly guide the attention back to the breath. This is the nature of the mind. Historically, the mind has done exactly whatever it has wanted to do. And now we are attempting to guide it, to train it. It usually resists this on some level. Our work is to return over and over again to the present moment, and in this way we train the mind.

This is called "mindfulness of breathing" and it develops the capacity to be settled and aware in the present. As the field of awareness expands, other senses are stimulated. There are sounds. Sounds arise in the field of awareness. Sounds are perceived. So we stay as best we can with the raw experience of hearing, rather than getting caught or lost in thoughts, stories, or judgments about what we may be hearing. Noting lightly the process in the background of our awareness. Using terms like "hearing, hearing" and then returning to the breath. Allowing the sounds to fade away and noticing this in the background, while in the foreground the attention is resting naturally on the breath. The in-breath . . . a slight pause . . . and the out-breath . . . just observing the breath.

As best as you can, staying with the breath as it enters and exits the body.

There may be sensations you would label as intense or uncomfortable, perhaps even painful. Just notice without resisting, without immediately trying to change the experience even when it is unpleasant. Maybe lightly asking questions like, "What do the sensations feel like? Do they change or stay the same? Is there a way to experience this discomfort without resisting or fighting it?"

Noticing any reactions that arise . . . and meeting whatever arises with kindness.

If there is tension . . . maybe softening those areas as best you can . . . just around the edges of that particular sensation. Just allowing, as best as you can, whatever has arisen to just *be*.

And now allowing the attention to shift from sensations to awareness of your thoughts. See if you can notice the very next thought that arises in the mind. Just watching each thought as it appears and passes away . . . . If you notice the mind getting lost in thought . . . notice that and simply, calmly, without criticism, return to the breath . . . over and over, simply returning . . . home . . . to the breath.

There may be emotions that are predominant in this moment . . . Maybe sadness? . . . Frustration? . . . Restlessness? Noticing . . . whatever is present to be noticed.

What does this emotion feel like? Where is it in the body? Maybe there are specific sensations that correspond to the emotion. Maybe tingling, heaviness, a change in the heartbeat, a change in the breathing, a contraction in the chest. Just see what can be noticed . . . seeing what is there and letting it *be*.

There are no distractions in this type of meditation, only something new to notice, to pay attention to . . . but not get lost in the content of.

In this way the full range of the present moment experience is able to unfold within the light of mindfulness . . . physical sensations . . . feelings . . . thoughts . . . mental states . . . moods . . . and intentions all reveal themselves.

Continuing on in this great adventure into the inner landscape of experience, keeping the attention soft and relaxed . . . alert and precise. Attempting to locate the feeling sense of the experience in contrast to the ideas, concepts, images, and stories about the experience.

Returning to the body again and again. What has arisen in this moment? And the next moment? And the next . . .

Noticing aversion . . . grasping . . . avoidance . . . wanting . . . and not becoming driven by any of them. Just allowing . . .

In this way, cultivating the ability to be mindful without interfering . . . judging . . . avoiding . . . or clinging so that the true nature of the experience can arise, leading to wisdom, compassion, and freedom . . .

Continuing this way until the bell sounds . . . (If you record this for yourself, let the recorder run for the amount of time you have chosen to sit and then ring a bell at the end.)

2. Body Scan

Body Scan is another form of mindfulness meditation. It is a guided meditation of great benefit for people suffering from chronic pain. It helps people in pain change the way they relate to their bodies and their condition by distinguishing between the felt-sense of the sensations described as pain and the mental aspect of aversion that creates the suffering. It is also used widely in various stress reduction programs. And, of course, it is tremendously useful to recovering addicts, who are trying to facilitate a deeper awareness of their bodies.

(Again, the ellipses—". . ."—denote pauses of a few beats. Longer pauses of five to ten beats are indicated by the word "Pause" in parentheses. Feel free to adapt these pauses to whatever suits your time requirements.)

Lying down in a position where you can be uninterrupted for about thirty minutes. Taking care in arranging pillows or cushions to support the body so that it is as comfortable as possible. Allowing attention to rest on the overall sensation of the body at ease and supported by the floor and the cushions. Noticing a sense of heaviness or contact where the body lies in repose; a sense of touch where the arms and hands lie on the body or the cushions. And just taking a few moments, now set your intention for this Body Scan . . . maybe agreeing to let go of the past and the future . . . letting sounds drift into the background of awareness . . . letting everything drift into the background . . . except for the body and the area that we are scanning at any particular time . . . . And once we scan over an area of the body, allow that part to "fade" from awareness . . . as the attention moves to the next body part . . . agreeing to meet whatever we find in the body with receptivity and openness . . . whether pleasant, unpleasant, or neutral . . .

Taking these first few moments to settle into the joy of just lying in a place at this point in time—in this moment. And, when ready, bringing attention to the sensations created by the breath entering and exiting the body . . . all by itself . . . in the present moment. The body breathes in the present moment . . . not the past . . . not the future . . . but now . . .

Noticing the rising and falling of the abdomen as the body breathes . . . without manipulating or changing the breath in any way . . . just allowing it to occur and noticing that. Maybe noticing an increasing sense of sinking into the cushions with each exhale; of allowing the body to just relax into the safety of the cushions.

When ready, allowing awareness and attention to travel down to the big toe of the left foot. You don't have to move it or wiggle it, just see if you can notice the presence of any physical sensations in this very specific area of the left big toe. Or notice the absence of sensation. Shifting attention now to the little toe of the left foot. What is there to be noticed? Then the toes in between . . . . Noticing the sense of contact between the toes of the left foot.

Moving now to the top of the left foot, the instep, noticing all the sensations in this area. Now the bottom of the left foot, the sole of the left foot.

Now taking a moment to bring attention more fully to the breath. And on the next inhale, let the breath enter the lungs and then continue down, all the way down to the left foot. And then exhaling and following the breath from the foot all the way up the leg to the abdomen, to the lungs, and then out of the body through the nostrils. Continue this way for a few breaths, breathing into and out of the left foot.

(Pause)

Now allowing attention to move up to the ankle of the left foot, as if shining a spotlight of awareness on the bones, ligaments, muscles, and tendons of the left foot. Just see if there are any sensations to be noticed in this area. Not forcing or searching for a sensation, just seeing whatever is there . . . or not. Now moving up to the shin of the left leg. Maybe there is a sense of contact here where clothing touches the shin of the left leg. Letting awareness slip around to the underside of the lower leg, to the calf of the left leg, noticing the sense of pressure or contact in this area.

Now allowing awareness to move up to the left knee. Noticing all the physical sensations in the left knee, all the while breathing into each area that we focus on as we scan through the body in this very deliberate, systematic, and patient way.

Shifting attention now to the thigh of the left leg, the top of the left thigh, and then allowing attention to slide around to the bottom of the left thigh, noticing the very strong sensation of weight, of contact, of pressure in this area at the bottom of the left thigh, and the left buttock area. Again, there is likely a very distinct sensation of weight, contact, and pressure.

And if at any time the mind wanders, simply guide attention back to whatever area is being scanned once becoming aware that the mind has drifted. No judgment . . . no story . . . just experience.

Now allowing attention to shift to the big toe of the right foot. Without moving it, breathe into and notice the sensations of the right big toe. Then the right little toe. Now all the toes in between, all the toes of the right foot. Are there any toes that are easier to feel than the rest? Are there any areas of the body where it is difficult to notice sensations? If so, just let awareness rest there briefly, without striving, and notice what the absence of sensation feels like.

Moving attention now to the top of the right foot, and the bottom of the right foot. Again breathing into and letting the breath travel—on the inhale—all the way to the bottom of the right foot; then on the exhale, all the way up the leg and out of the body through the lungs and the nostrils. Breathe into the right foot for a couple of breaths in this way.

(Pause)

Now allowing the spotlight of awareness to focus on the right ankle, and then moving up to the right shin. What is here to be noticed? Slide around to the right calf area and all the sensations present there. Observing contact, pressure, and weight.

Moving up to the right knee, and noticing . . .

If there are any areas where discomfort, or anything that might be described as pain, is present try to just observe these intense sensations without trying to push them away or have any particular sensation *not* be present. If anything, just breathe into the area of intense sensation . . . as if the intense sensation were absorbing the in-breath. And then, on the exhale, let go. But let go with the mind, let go of the story, of the desire for the experience to be something other than what it is right now, and perhaps locating the "edges" of the intense sensation, and then moving on.

Allowing attention to focus on the top of the right thigh, and then on the sense of contact, of pressure, and weight in the area at the bottom of the right thigh and the right buttock.

When ready, shifting attention to the waist and hip area. Noticing whatever is there to be noticed, and breathing—with mindful awareness—into the waist and hip area . . . attention shifting around to the lower back area . . . that hollow area perhaps supported by cushions? . . . noticing if there is any tension or tightness in this area . . . and, when ready, moving up to the middle of the back . . . in the center of the spine . . . and resting there . . . allowing the breath into this area . . . and moving into the upper back . . . the shoulder blade area . . . sensing that strong sensation of weight in the shoulder blades . . . and then attention sliding back down to the lower back and the waist area again . . .

Shifting attention to the lower abdomen. Noticing the rising and falling . . . the sense of spaciousness in this area of the body; and the ribs expanding and contracting with the breath . . . . Moving up, when ready, to the center of the chest, the heart area. See if you can detect the sensations of the heart, deep in the body as it nourishes the body. And the upper chest and collarbone area. What is there? What is there to be noticed?

And, when ready, letting attention travel down the left arm . . . all the way to the fingers of the left hand. Noticing the thumb and fingers of the left hand, the distinct sensations present in each finger; the sense of contact between the fingers . . . on the finger tips as they contact the floor, the body, or the cushion. Noticing the palm of the left hand and the back of the left hand. Moving into the wrist of the left hand, and—breathing—further up to the left forearm, the left elbow. Letting go of the elbow and shifting awareness to the upper portion of the left arm. What is there to be noticed in the biceps, the triceps of the left arm? Then moving attention into the shoulder. Are there any areas of tension or tightness? Of holding? Contraction? Just noticing. Across the chest and down the right arm, breathing into the fingers of the right hand—exhaling and releasing— . . . allowing . . . sensing all the points of contact in the right hand, and the right palm, the back of the right hand. And moving into the wrist area. The muscles, tendons, and ligaments of the right wrist.

And, when ready, shifting attention up to the forearm of the right arm, the elbow, then the upper portion of the right arm, the biceps and triceps of the right arm, and the right shoulder. What is present in the right shoulder? The right shoulder fading from awareness as the spotlight of attention focuses on the throat and the front of the neck. Sliding around to the back of the neck, the sides of the neck, feeling whatever is there to be felt. Moving into the area where the neck attaches to the head, in the back. Is there any tension or tightness? Fading up the back of the head, can you feel the hair on the head? Focusing on the left side of the head, and the left ear, shifting to the forehead. Then over to the right ear, and down the jaw line to the chin . . . the lips . . . and the nose. Paying particular attention to the nostril area. Can you feel the sensations as the breath enters and exits the nostrils? Perhaps noticing the difference in temperature? Then moving over to the left cheekbone, and the right cheekbone, up to the right eye socket area, the eyelid of the right eye, the eyebrow. And on to the left eyebrow, the left eye socket area, the left eyelid. Up over the forehead to the top of the head, lingering here at the **"Bai Hui,"** what the Chinese call the "hundred meeting place"—an area of great power and receptivity, of connectivity. Are there any sensations here?

And now after scanning the entire body this way, just resting and breathing, seeing, sensing the whole body . . . connected, integrated, alive—the whole body breathing as one complete living organism . . . the whole body, breathing.

And, when ready, just slowly wiggling the toes and fingers, maybe stretching lightly. And now gently opening the eyes, seeing if you can bring this open, receptive awareness to bear on all that enters the field of awareness through the sense of sight. After a while, slowly, mindfully rising, paying close attention to the sensation of movement as the body rises mindfully . . .

3. Walking Meditation

The Body Scan is only one of the ways in which we can experience a more embodied presence. There are many others. Walking meditation is another way of focusing the mind in the body. This way involves movement, which makes it an excellent transitional practice for someone accomplished with traditional sitting meditation or Body Scan. Both of these are practiced in relative stillness. The question arises, "What happens when we add movement?" Or, "How do I apply mindfulness to movement?"

This can be tricky because much of the movements and actions we perform on a daily basis have a strong habitual tendency. We do many actions over and over again on a daily basis, so not much attention is needed for us to perform them. Walking is one such action. When we were babies and first attempting to walk, it required much attention and mindful effort of the body and mind. In a relatively short period of time the body was able to "walk" fairly competently with a minimum of conscious attention. When the intention is formed to move from one place to another, the body simply reacts to accomplish this task.

Mindful walking or walking meditation is in effect a return to the time when we had to pay close attention to what occurs when we walk. Now that we are grown we can really feel an appreciation for the miracle of walking upright and balanced, given all the processes and laws of nature that have to be coordinated for walking to occur. To do that we have to slow down a bit to feel and notice the intricacies of muscle coordination, balance, and gravity that are at play when we move the body through space. This sense of "knowing" and feeling the body's position in space, whether statically or in motion, is called **"proprioception."** Science actually regards proprioception as another one of our senses, indicating that we have more than five senses. If proprioception is lost, the sense of the body is nonexistent. You can see how cultivating proprioception as well as **"interoception"**—the sense of knowing how your body is feeling from the inside—is valuable. Interoception is an internal, embodied feeling, whereas proprioception is the sense we have of our body in our environment. Mindfulness practices are about putting a great deal of attention on a sense of the body as a whole, while sitting, lying, or moving. This is a skill we can learn—to be fully aware of our body, both internally and in relation to our environment, and to sustain this awareness over time. In essence, it is about being present in a very distinct, physical and mental way; in touch and connected to what we are doing, why we are doing it, and the effect of what we are doing on other people and the environment around us. Walking practice is an excellent place to start.

I once met a Thai Forest monk who placed such high value on walking practice that he always started his students with walking meditation. Only once their mindfulness was sufficiently established would he graduate them to traditional mindful sitting meditation. So don't underestimate or take lightly the value of this simple practice. I will offer some very basic instructions for walking meditation, but it is important to realize that this particular practice varies widely, depending on who is teaching it and from what discipline his or her practice was developed.

Walking mindfully is an excellent way to connect to the sense of how the body feels when it moves in a particular way—with no purpose other than to appreciate and experience the action itself, and without concern for a particular destination, result, or mental state. The purpose is to just notice the raw sensation, as it is in the body while walking.

It is helpful to find a place, ideally outdoors in nature, where you can be relatively undisturbed for the duration of the practice. The duration is to be determined by you. It could be ten minutes, a full hour, or even longer if your life affords you that privilege. It is advisable to practice for a preset length of time, at least in the beginning, so you don't get caught up in thinking about time unnecessarily while walking. You will be free to just walk. When walking, just walk. Simple enough, right?

Usually you pick a path approximately ten to fifteen feet in length. This is where you will walk for the duration of this practice session. It can change in the future, but for this meditation you will remain here. If other people are present, pick a place that doesn't intersect or cross another person's "path." Then you simply walk back and forth on the path. When you come to the end, you stop briefly, then turn around and walk in the other direction. Choosing a limited, predefined area like this to walk in is important, as opposed to just wandering around, because the mind will be less likely to slip into thinking about preferences as to where to walk and for how long. In this way, the problem-solving part of the mind can settle once the timeframe and route are established, and you have completed a few repetitions.

Circles are sometimes used but they have a disadvantage. If others are walking on the same circle, one can become preoccupied with constantly adjusting or "worrying" about one's pace in relation to others on the circle. Also, the stopping at the end of a straight path provides an opportunity to better "catch" the mind when it is wandering. The circle, because it is continuous, makes this a little more difficult.

Next is pace. I have seen practitioners walk extremely slowly. I have seen others walk very fast almost like they are walking a race. Somewhere in the middle of these extremes is generally good. It should be a pace that is comfortable for you, offering a sense of ease, and the ability to really notice the physical sensations in the process. If you tend to walk fast in your everyday life, like I do, then slow is a good discipline to practice. If you are drowsy and your energy leans toward the subdued side, then a brisker pace could help invigorate you. And you can always change your pace during an individual walking meditation session as awareness of your mind-state changes.

Once you have found your pace, you can let your attention settle into the body. Bringing a sense of awareness to the body as it moves through space. Inviting the attention to drop down into the feet and lower legs. We use the alternating movement of the feet stepping as the focus, or the object of our meditation. We place mindful and deliberate attention on the sensations present as we step and touch each foot upon the earth. Bring open, receptive awareness of the process and the feelings present. We notice the pressure as the weight shifts unto a foot and the release as the weight lifts off of the opposite foot. The body weight shifts smoothly onto and off of each foot.

One technique that I love is gentle noting of the process of walking. This is especially useful if the mind is very active and unsettled. We very simply and softly, in the mind, when lifting the rear foot, note lifting. Then, as the foot moves forward, note moving. And as the foot settles on the ground, note placing. Then, as the body shifts onto the forward leg and foot, note shifting. Then simply repeat this for each foot. In this way we try to bring the mind to bear on the contraction and release of muscles necessary to perform the movement. And then, when and if the mind settles down or the noting becomes cumbersome, simply drop it. Instead, rely on the attention firmly established and focus on the miraculous process of walking effortlessly and smoothly in space. Aware and connected to the body in a way we may not have ever experienced.

4. Mindful Movement

In review, we have learned about the value of mindfulness practice through the modalities of Sitting Meditation, Body Scan, and Walking Meditation. Now we will learn how to incorporate mindfulness into an exercise routine—not your average, run-of-the-mill exercise routine—but one steeped in tradition and full of proven benefits beyond what are typically achieved with simple exercise. We will learn how to use Chi Kung as a vehicle for promoting mindfulness and as a process for experiencing mindfulness. The alpha and omega if you will, with the actualized result of complete well-being in the physical realm of our recovery.

Recently I have started to incorporate a more liberal use of Chi Kung practice as a basis for Mindful Movement. Practicing in this way focuses more on the direct experience of the movements where we are mindfully present to the process and felt sense, with less attention on performing the movements exactly right. The benefit of this type of Mindful Movement is that it's a more relaxed process, free of the tensions and the urge to perfect movements common in participants of traditional Chi Kung classes. It is very easy to get drawn out of the body and into the head when trying to learn Chi Kung or Tai Chi Chuan. We know that these exercises are performed in a certain manner for a certain result and we strive for correct form—sometimes too strongly in the beginning. What happens as a result is that we lose or never attain a high level of mindful presence in the body, which is actually necessary for a rewarding Chi Kung practice. So I am including guided Mindful Movement here to assist in this area. Once mindfulness becomes present and you are comfortable in this relaxed manner, you are more likely to continue mindfully when attempting the more disciplined traditional Chi Kung teachings. The following is a series that I have used while co-teaching a Stress Reduction program. I'm including it due to the overwhelmingly positive response it has received.

Just as with the other guided exercises, you can have someone read this to you in a calm, relaxed voice or you can record it yourself for playback. Of course the eventual goal is to be able to practice without guidance, simply trusting your own intuition, knowledge, and feeling sense within the body. There will be no photos or illustrations in this section for precisely this reason. Just do, just feel, just be. Mindfully moving, with awareness and paying careful attention to how the body is responding to the movements, so that injury or overworking can be avoided. Have fun and remember to smile if the body becomes inclined in this direction.

(As before, the ellipses—". . ."—denote pauses of a few beats. Longer pauses of five to ten beats are indicated by the word "Pause" in parentheses. Feel free to adapt these pauses to whatever suits your time requirements.)

Just stand easily with the feet placed about shoulder distance apart. Relaxing the knees and extending your body upright into a dignified and noble posture, as if a cord were pulling gently up from the crown of the head . . . . Coming into the body with your attention, noticing as best as you can what is present in the way of raw physical sensation by simply standing upright in space. Recognizing the miraculous involvement of a multitude of physical processes necessary to keep you balanced and upright in gravity. And trying, as best as you can, without forcing, to notice some of these processes through sensations. You might feel a sense of contact where the feet are placed on the earth, a sense of connectedness, perhaps a feeling of being grounded and rooted in the earth, to the planet itself. Maybe noticing muscle contractions as they perform microscopic adjustments in every moment just to keep you standing. Maybe there is some discomfort or tension or tightness someplace in the body. Notice this, without needing to change the sensation in any way. Likewise if the sensation is very intense, something we may even describe as painful. Just look. Just notice. Just feel, without having to do anything . . .

Now, allowing the hands to come to rest on the lower abdomen . . . allowing the fingers to feel the rise and fall of the lower abdomen, as the body breathes. Air is entering and exiting the body all by itself with no help needed from you. In fact . . . let go of the desire, or the propensity to manipulate the breath in any way. Just feel it . . . . Resting here for as long as is comfortable, to elicit a strong sense of the body breathing, and of the feelings present here in the center of our being, the core . . . . Then, when you are ready, allowing the attention to drop down from the abdomen, through the legs and into the feet. Still aware of the body breathing, placing a more focused attention on the sensations as they exist in the feet . . . right now.

Again, feeling the minute movements in the feet, the sense of connectedness, the root. And now, just for fun . . . for the sheer enjoyment of feeling the subtle distribution of weight and balance in the feet . . . start to manipulate where the weight shifts on the bottom of the feet and noticing the consequential changes that occur in the process . . .

When you are ready, shifting the weight forward slightly onto the balls of the feet and noticing the sense of fullness or heaviness that arises in the front of the legs . . . a feeling of fullness, and the backs of the legs feeling rather empty and light . . . interesting? And then very slowly, very slightly shift the weight backward onto the heels, and feeling the backs of the legs get heavy and full . . . and the front of the legs now feeling empty and light . . .

Perhaps shifting the weight onto one leg . . . most of the weight balanced on one leg. And that leg feeling full and heavy and the opposite leg feeling light, empty, soft, open . . . . And then shifting the weight to the other side . . . and noticing with great attention the change . . . the various sensations moving and adapting.

(Pause)

And now, with attention resting on the soles of the feet, on the bottoms of the feet, begin to experiment with random patterns of weight distribution . . . moving the body gently, slowly in circles, figure eight patterns, side to side, front to back . . . totally at the whim of the mind . . . with no expectations, with no reason or plan other than the pure, raw experience of the body in motion . . . just feeling what it feels like to move the body in space, with subtle attention grounded in the feet . . . feeling that strong connection to the earth . . . that sense of rootedness in the feet . . . the body above the feet soft and supple, relaxed, swaying . . . however the mind desires the body to move, at the whim of the mind . . . like seaweed at the whim of the ocean's currents . . . strongly rooted on the ocean floor . . . secure, grounded, connected . . . and the upper part of the plant relaxed and swaying . . . supported by the water around it . . . . The nature of water is such that it supports the seaweed . . . yet allows it to flow and respond to the movement of currents in the ocean . . . soft, receptive . . . ever lengthening upward toward the life-giving sunlight on the surface of the ocean . . . just moving softly.

(Pause)

Perhaps a large fish swims by and causes the currents in the water to increase in strength . . . the water responding to the large fish swimming through it and the seaweed responding to the stronger currents with faster and bigger movements, yet still flowing . . . and still rooted strongly to the ocean floor . . . and when the fish moves on . . . the slower action of the water causes the movements to soften, causing the seaweed to respond in kind . . . movements slowing down . . . supported by the ocean water's viscosity . . . ever quieter and slower . . . soft and receptive . . . smaller and smaller movements until the body returns to relative stillness . . . feet rooted . . . body soft, relaxed, and still . . . arms resting by the sides . . . attention settled in the body.

(Pause)

And now . . . when ready, letting the hands come to rest on the lower abdomen, in stillness.

Beginning the joint lubrication exercises. Let the arms rise up in front of the body and begin to circle the wrists, trying as best as you can to get a full range of motion . . . with attention resting on the wrists as they circle, noticing whatever is present, just in the wrist joints, as the movement continues . . . and then reversing the direction of the wrist rotations . . .

Now moving to the elbow joints, with the arms out to the side . . . try as best as you can to isolate just the elbow joints as they are rotating outward, attention focused on the elbows as the forearms rotate like windmills . . . and then reverse, with the forearms rotating inward . . .

what do the elbows feel like right now, as this movement engages them . . . as the synovial fluid is stimulated and activated?

Now moving up to the shoulder joints, rotating both arms forward like windmills . . . pivoting on the shoulder joints . . . as much movement as the body allows . . . always redirecting attention back to the body . . . back to the specific area we are manipulating . . . and now reversing the arms to rotate backward . . . is anything different? Paying attention to the shoulder joints . . . and now letting the arms relax at your sides . . .

And, when you are ready, gently rotating the neck . . . nice and slow . . . mindful of any pressure in the cervical vertebrae . . . and adjusting accordingly . . . slowly stretching to the sides and forward . . . letting the neck hang forward . . . continuing in one direction at your own pace.

(Pause)

And then reversing . . . slowly continuing the mindful exploration of the neck in the opposite direction.

(Pause)

And relax, allowing the head to balance between the shoulders . . . eyes gazing forward . . .

Moving into the upper chest and shoulder blade area . . . raising the arms up in front of the chest with one arm above the other but not touching . . . feeling that gentle stretch in the shoulder blades as you do so. And then, when you are ready, pulling your arms away from each other . . . toward the back . . . elbows up . . . with hands formed in soft fists . . . feeling the chest opening . . . and stretching . . . slowly with soft, small movements . . . as much stretch as the body allows at this time . . . increasing the stretch as you move the arms backward and then forward . . . crossing one above the other in front of the chest . . . gently increasing the range of motion as the body permits more movement . . . always listening to the body and the multitude of sensations that develop from the movement . . . continuing on your own . . . with the breath leading the movement . . . breathing into the stretching sensations in the upper chest and back . . .

(Pause)

And relaxing, with the arms at your sides.

Now rolling the shoulders . . . alternating one shoulder and then the other . . . rotating forward . . . again with as much motion as the body allows in this moment . . . feeling, sensing, experiencing what it feels like . . . all the complicated signals and coordinated systems in the body that are necessary just to perform this simple shoulder roll movement.

(Pause)

And, when you are ready, reversing to backward shoulder rolls . . . again alternating between one shoulder and then the other.

(Pause)

Noticing the opening and stretching in the ribcage as the whole body balances and adjusts to perform the backward rotation of the shoulder joints . . . and continuing on your own . . . at your own pace . . . allowing the breath to lead.

(Pause)

And relaxing again, with your arms by your sides, in stillness.

Now moving into the waist region . . . there is much to be observed and listened to in this region . . . so be mindful and careful . . . always beginning with small and slow movements . . . and perhaps staying with small, very gentle side-to-side movements if the body is resisting due to stiffness or previous injury to this area . . . being patient and waiting to increase the range of motion only when the body softens enough to allow it . . . and now from side to side, twist the upper body from one side to the other . . . allowing the arms to hang loosely and sway in rhythm to the slow side-to-side pivoting or raising the arms slightly with soft fists as we did with the upper chest stretches . . . gently and softly . . . side to side . . . not unlike a washing machine on a very gentle cycle . . . feeling, sensing, experiencing that nice stretch occurring in the lower spine area . . . and the releasing as the body shifts to the other side . . . back and forth . . . with complete awareness and attention to any sensations that are developing in this very complicated area of the body.

(Pause)

And continuing on your own, at your own pace . . . just feeling.

(Pause)

And, when you are ready, slowing down and returning to stillness with your arms resting by your sides . . .

Moving into the upper torso rotation.

(Pause)

While keeping your hips relatively stationary, rotate the upper torso around in a circle as if there were a ball in the hip area . . . remember to start with small, tight circles and then spiraling out into a fuller range of motion, again, as the body allows . . . there might be many sensations in the lower spine area as the movement flexes and stretches and activates the ligaments, tendons, muscles, and bones of the lower back . . . so be very mindful and move with care and great friendliness to the body . . . perhaps letting go of any preconceived levels of ability or flexibility . . . and instead focusing and moving with whatever is present today . . . in this moment.

(Pause)

And now reversing the movements in the opposite direction . . . moving with the same attention, care, and kindness as before . . . always looking . . . always listening . . . feeling . . . and noticing . . . be curious about whatever shows up in the realm of physical sensations . . . continuing at your own pace.

(Pause)

And after completing approximately the same amount of rotations in both directions, come to stillness again . . . always returning . . . always stopping and resting with an increasing sense of poise and awareness . . .

And now, standing with the feet approximately shoulder distance apart, prepare to lubricate the hip joints by imagining a circle that forms around the outside edges of the feet . . . now, when you are ready, begin to trace this imaginary circle with a rotation of the pelvis forward, then to the side, then backward, then to the other side . . . in a manner that manipulates the hip joints through a nice range of motion . . . in a circle . . . remembering to move slowly and to pay attention to what is showing up as you perform this movement . . . continuing on your own . . . breathing into the hip joints . . . breathing into the movement . . . allowing the hips to open to the movement at their own pace . . . never forcing . . . or criticizing . . . instead being receptive, open . . . moving in complete acceptance of whatever the body allows in this moment, in this movement.

(Pause)

And, when you are ready, reversing the rotations in the opposite direction . . . continue for approximately the same amount of time in this direction . . . on your own . . . at your own pace.

(Pause)

When finished, simply come to stillness with the arms by your sides . . .

Moving into the knee lubrication exercises, standing with the feet close together, bend the knees and place both hands on the knees . . . one hand on each knee . . . be mindful not to rest your weight on the knees . . . just support them with gentle pressure from the hands . . . then begin to rotate the knees together, in the same direction, very slowly, in small circles . . . slower is better with the knees . . . giving the kneecaps time to settle and adjust to the movement as the fingers support them lightly . . . when you are ready, reverse and continue in the opposite direction for the same amount of time . . . listening to . . . and noticing the sensations as they are, without adding any ideas . . . or stories . . . or judgments to whatever is occurring.

(Pause)

And coming to stillness, with your arms by your sides.

And, when you are ready, bringing attention to the ankle joints . . . acknowledging the hard work that the ankles perform for the body . . . supporting the body through any upright activity . . . standing . . . walking . . . running . . . all the weight of the body bearing down on these often underappreciated joints.

(Pause)

Let us take time to provide care and kindness, and gratitude to these humble servants of the body . . . begin by first shifting the weight onto one foot and balancing the opposite foot on the big toe, off to the side in a comfortable position . . . once balanced and stable . . . begin to rotate the ankle . . . pivoting on the big toe . . . as best as you can . . . while breathing into the ankle joint . . . allowing the ankle to move through a full range of motion relative to whatever is present in terms of comfort . . . balance . . . and stability.

(Pause)

And then reversing the rotations in the opposite direction.

(Pause)

And, when you are ready, placing the rotating foot securely on the ground and shifting the weight to that foot, in preparation for rotating the opposite ankle in the same fashion . . . with the same level of concern . . . of care . . . of appreciation . . . continuing on your own.

(Pause)

And reversing direction.

(Pause)

When you have completed approximately the same amount of rotations on that ankle, stop and stand with the feet about shoulder width apart . . . with the arms hanging by the sides . . . and close the eyes briefly . . . journey inward . . . focus the attention inside the body and see what is available to be noticed after having completed the lubrication exercises . . . what do the joints feel like? Is there anything about them that can be noticed? If not, that is fine too . . . just observe . . .

And, as we stand here in this neutral posture . . . just standing . . . sensing . . . being . . . aware of the energy and sensations within the body . . . and without . . . aware and connected to the energy in the air . . . the earth . . . the sky . . . the wind . . . the sun . . . all the energy of nature is supporting and nurturing us in our lives.

(Pause)

Bring your hands once again to rest lightly on the lower abdomen, slightly below the belly button, as before . . . just resting the hands there on this Tan Tien area . . . feeling the subtle expansion of this area as the breath enters the body . . . and then the collapsing . . . the relaxing of this area as the breath exits the body . . . inhaling and exhaling . . . the breath moving all by itself . . . effortlessly.

(Pause)

Just allowing . . . just breathing . . . just sensing the breath in the body.

(Pause)

And, when you are ready, letting the arms move to the sides and then raising them upward in front of the body as you inhale . . . in coordination with the breath . . . the arms rising to shoulder height, as if a fishing line were attached to each wrist, drawing the arms up . . . upon reaching shoulder height the exhalation begins and the arms lower slowly . . . in coordination with the exhalation, until they reach the hips . . . attention focused on the sensations in the arms . . . the body . . . the feet . . . as energy from the earth is drawn up through the feet by the drawing movement of the arms rising . . . and then this chi . . . this energy . . . settles and collects in the Tan Tien area . . . inhale, the arms rising . . . exhale the arms floating down . . . as if on a cloud . . . continue on your own, at your own pace . . . allowing the breath to lead . . . as the body becomes rooted and grounded to the earth.

(Pause)

After completing several repetitions, let the arms come to rest at the sides with the backs of the hands facing forward . . . with the arms slightly away from the sides of the body . . . shoulders relaxed, in this Wu Chi . . . empty . . . nothing posture . . . in harmony . . . connected . . . and calm . . .

And, when you are ready, turn the palms up as the arms begin to rise up and out to the sides in coordination with a long deep inhalation . . . the hands meeting above the head as the exhalation begins and the arms lower in front of the body . . . in coordination with the exhalation and resting on the lower abdomen at the end of the exhalation . . . and repeat again with the arms rising out to the sides and up in a nice circular motion as you inhale . . . and down the front of the body on the exhale . . . gathering chi from heaven and placing it in the Tan

Tien . . . what is here to be noticed? What can be felt? Continue on your own for a few repetitions . . . remembering to let go of efforts toward exactness . . . toward perfection . . . focusing instead on allowing the breath to lead the movements and maintaining awareness on sensations in the body . . . have fun . . . be loose . . . be light . . . be mindful of the joy of movement . . . and at the end of the next repetition come to stillness with the arms at your sides . . .

And, when you are ready, turning the palms upward and moving the hands in front of the pelvis area . . . the groin area . . . with the fingertips facing each other . . . and on an inhale, let the breath draw the hands up in front of the body to the heart level . . . at this point the hands turn over to face outward in a pushing position . . . hold the breath slightly as the arms straighten and the hands move forward to arm's-length . . . then you can begin to exhale as the arms open to the sides . . . when they reach the point at which the arms are extending outward from each side of the body, allow them to float down to the sides, as if on clouds . . . continue on your own, at your own pace . . . determined by the breath as it is in the body right now.

(Pause)

Unifying and combining chi from heaven and earth . . . connecting.

(Pause)

And at the end of the next repetition, come to stillness with the arms resting at the sides in the Wu Chi posture . . .

Moving into the looking back posture . . . let your hands rest once again on the Tan Tien . . . the lower abdomen area . . . feeling what is here to be felt . . . and, when you are ready, allowing the arms to open out as you inhale . . . arms opening and twisting as they move backward . . . opening the chest . . . and pulling the shoulder blades together . . . the head turning to one side or the other, nice and even . . . and the eyes pulling toward that side in an effort to see over that shoulder . . . ahhhh . . . what does this feel like? And then, having completed the inhalation . . . the head turns back to face forward, and the arms start to move in a big, circular, grasping motion toward the Tan Tien as the body exhales . . . hands resting on the lower abdomen . . . and inhale . . . opening, moving the arms back . . . twisting the arms slightly so that the tendons and ligaments are activated . . . looking back . . . and exhaling again as the arms gather chi . . . gather energy from the air in front of you and place it in the Tan Tien . . . continuing on your own, at your own pace . . . allowing your breath to lead . . . to move into the arms . . . allowing the chest, the heart to open . . . feeling that connectedness as the arms are splayed back in this open, receptive, and trusting posture . . . allowing the heart to connect to all beings, to all things . . . the connection is already there . . . we are simply acknowledging it . . . recognizing it . . . supporting it . . . feeling it . . . awakening to it.

(Pause)

And at the end of the next repetition, coming to stillness with the arms by your sides . . .

And now, when you are ready, moving into the Drawing the Bow posture . . . moving the feet a little farther apart . . . a little farther than shoulder width, if that is comfortable for you . . . always checking, always noticing just what it is that the body will allow at this point in time . . . in this moment . . . with the upper body erect as one arm draws across the thigh-pelvis area in front of the body . . . the opposite arm extending out from the side with the index finger pointing upward . . . inhaling as the lower hand comes up to meet the other hand and begins the Drawing the Bow motion . . . shoulders in line with the hips, as the drawing arm pulls back . . . opening the chest area . . . still inhaling . . . a great big inhale . . . and then, when the arm has pulled all the way back . . . exhaling deeply and sinking into the posture and repeating on the other side . . . allowing the other arm to scoop and move across the body as the opposite arm extends with index finger pointing skyward . . . and once meeting . . . pulling back slowly . . . completely inflating the lungs to the maximum capacity . . . full . . . full . . . full . . . drawing the arm back . . . and release . . . exhaling . . . and sinking . . . completely exhaling . . . emptying the lungs . . . completely . . . continuing on your own, alternating Drawing the Bow from side to side . . . letting the breath lead the movement . . . focusing on completely filling the lungs . . . and completely emptying the lungs . . . full and empty . . . yin and yang . . . noticing the sensations that arise . . . what does it feel like to fill the lungs this way? What does it feel like to empty the lungs this way?

(Pause)

And, at the end of the next set of repetitions . . . allowing the arms to come to rest at your sides . . . the body resting in stillness.

(Pause)

Next, moving into the Embrace the World posture. Move the feet in so that they are closer together than for the last exercise . . . about shoulder distance apart . . . begin by inhaling as the arms cross in front of the chest. Remember to inhale with a long slow, breath . . . breathing into the movement. As the arms continue to move up from in front of the chest . . . still crossed . . . to in front of the face . . . and then beginning to separate as they continue in the circular motion above the head, but forward. Now begin the exhale as the arms continue the movement, circling out to the sides and down on the exhale . . . and then repeating . . . inhaling up . . . arms crossing . . . rising . . . opening above the head . . . exhaling and descending in arcs . . . out and down . . . and then up again . . . continuing in this circular rotation the arms, with an added crossing of the arms in front of the chest . . . inhaling upward . . . and exhaling downward . . . the arms soft and relaxed . . . as if floating . . . letting go of precision . . . letting go of perfection . . . just flowing . . . just breathing . . . and . . . flowing . . . continuing on your own . . . letting the breath carry the movement . . . letting the breath lead the movement . . . letting the breath *be* the movement . . . seamless . . . connected . . . alive.

(Pause)

And, at the end of the next repetition, letting the arms come down to rest at your sides . . .

And, when you are ready, widening your stance to just past shoulder width and crouching down with the hands placed just above the knees with the fingers on the inside of the thighs, just above the knees . . . supporting the upper body . . . the back flat like a table . . . inhale and bow the back so that the tailbone turns up slightly and the head bends backward, as you crouch slightly . . . the back is U-shaped . . . like the cow posture in yoga . . . only the hands are on the legs instead of the floor . . . and then on the exhale, bending the back downward, head coming forward and down . . . like a cat stretching . . . and then flat again . . . taking time to catch the breath if the rhythm is off . . . and then inhaling . . . arching the back up . . . tailbone up . . . head back . . . and exhaling . . . head falling forward and down . . . back arching up . . . tailbone relaxing . . . and release . . . returning to a flat back . . . like a table . . . pause slightly and then inhaling again, stomach dropping down . . . tailbone back . . . and head back . . . as much as the body allows . . . and then exhaling . . . only this time, rising up slowly from the tailbone, through the lower spine, thoracic region, on up through the cervical area . . . restacking the vertebrae . . . one at a time, until the posture is upright . . . and now beginning to rotate around in a circle as if there were a ball in the hip-pelvis area . . . opening and closing the ribs alternately . . . making sure not to hold the breath . . . just breathe normally, with no coordination between the breath and the movements . . . letting attention focus on the internal organs . . . on the flexing and twisting of the lower spine . . . only what the body allows . . . listening . . . noticing . . . what does it feel like to manipulate the organs in this way? Hands resting on the belly . . . helping to feel the sensations . . . lightly touching . . . letting gravity and the circular undulations perform a nice gentle internal massage for the vital organs . . . paying attention to the organs . . . massaging the organs.

(Pause)

And reversing . . . continuing in the opposite direction with the same level of attention and focus . . . seeing it all . . . feeling it all . . . just the pure experience of movement . . . inside and outside the body . . . as you like . . . for the same amount of time as the other direction.

(Pause)

And, when you are ready, coming slowly to stillness with the arms moving to your sides and the feet angling in until they are approximately shoulder width apart . . . and pause in the stillness.

(Pause)

For the next movement, called Touching the Toes, begin by inhaling as the arms rise out to each side until about shoulder height . . . and then holding the breath slightly as the arms circle around to in front of the body with the palms facing each other . . . arms extended . . . as if holding a ball . . . and then beginning the exhale . . . through the mouth as the body slowly begins to bend toward the floor, with the arms extending down and hanging . . . bend only to a point of comfort for you . . . listening closely to any clues the body may provide as far as what it is capable of right now . . . or maybe bending the knees to soften the stretch . . . just notice . . . once bent over let the arms hang freely as you inhale . . . and then touching the sides of the feet with the fingertips as the exhale begins . . . and then rising upward with the body, with the fingers gliding along the backs of the legs, until reaching the kidneys where they stop and support that area as the body bends backward slightly . . . feeling a mild stretch as you do so . . . and then relaxing the arms down at your sides.

(Pause)

And centering . . . noticing as you stand . . . what is here to be seen? To be learned? To be known? And, when you are ready, beginning again . . . inhaling with the arms moving up, extending out to the sides . . . and then holding . . . arms moving toward each other in front of you . . . and then exhaling . . . bending over slowly . . . and hanging . . . inhaling . . . and rising . . . fingers caressing the sides of the feet, the back of the legs . . . continuing . . . exhaling . . . hands supporting the kidneys . . . back arched slightly . . . exhale finished and relaxing . . . paying close attention . . . as you stand in stillness . . . what is here now? And continuing at your own pace . . . allowing the breath to lead . . . as many repetitions as is comfortable . . . stopping and resting when the need arises . . . connected and in sync . . . the mind and the body as one.

(Pause) . . . (Pause)

And, at the end of the next cycle of movements . . . just standing . . . noble . . . relaxed . . . alive . . .

With attention firmly grounded in the bottoms of both feet, gently turn one foot out to the side in a T-stance . . . adjust the foot position to ensure a comfortable stance . . . now facing to the side from where you started . . . and begin to focus on the multitude of sensations as they are in the feet and lower legs . . . just standing in this posture . . . begin to notice how the sensations change with only slight movements of the upper body . . . and then larger movements as you shift the weight very slowly and slightly between the back foot and the front foot . . . a slight rocking motion . . . forward and back . . . be mindful of the position of the knee in this exercise and be sure it doesn't extend past the toes of the front foot as the weight shifts onto that foot . . . noticing the exchange between full and empty in the legs as weight shifts onto or off of that particular leg . . . the feet firmly rooted and connected to the earth no matter where the weight is shifted . . . still subtle changes in sensation in the soles of the feet as the body adjusts to balance itself throughout the movements . . . just moving . . . just shifting . . . back . . . and forth . . . rocking . . . forward . . . and back . . . at your own pace.

(Pause)

And now incorporating the arms and hands . . . the arms rise up in front of the upper body with the elbows bent so that the hands can face the body when the weight is back and turn away from the body when the weight shifts forward . . . very soft . . . very light . . . without tension . . . as best as you can . . . and the breath leads once again . . . exhaling as the weight and the body shifts forward onto the front foot with the hands facing out . . . and inhaling . . . hands turning toward the body when the weight shifts onto the back leg . . . continue on your own in this manner . . . exhaling . . . moving forward . . . hands outward . . . giving, sharing, offering . . . and hands toward the body while inhaling . . . absorbing, allowing, receiving . . . the universal principle of reciprocity at work . . . yin and yang . . . giving . . . and . . . receiving.

(Pause)

Balanced . . . flowing . . . rocking . . . calming . . . letting go through the naturally relaxing nature of the movement . . . accentuating the rocking sensation if you like by lifting the forward toes slightly when the weight is back . . . and lifting the back heel when the weight is forward . . . keeping the balance . . . emphasizing the soothing nature of the rocking motion . . . taking us back . . . back to that primal sensation of comfort and security when we were rocked as infants . . . connected . . . and secure . . . safe.

(Pause)

And now turning to rock in the opposite direction, with the other leg leading . . . shifting as seamlessly and effortlessly as possible . . . letting go of exactness . . . of perfection . . . just moving . . . just feeling the joy of movement . . . giving . . . offering . . . sharing . . . and . . . absorbing . . . allowing . . . receiving . . . inhaling and . . . exhaling . . .

continuing on your own . . . at your own pace . . . for an equal amount of time . . . rocking.

(Pause) . . . (Pause)

And, when you are ready, turning the foot so that both feet face forward again and the arms relax at your sides . . .

(Pause)

Now moving the feet close together for Great Bird Flaps Its Wings On an Island In the Middle of a Lake . . . Chinese masters of old were very astute observers, particularly of natural environments. One of the things they noticed, and that I touched upon earlier, was that certain animals were very efficient at expending and conserving energy—large birds being one such animal. Large birds like cranes or geese have a great deal of body mass and require a lot of energy to propel themselves smoothly through the air. Yet they are able to do this almost effortlessly, and for long distances without fatigue. This indicates a very advanced relationship with energy and how it can be efficiently conserved and expended. This is the idea behind this next exercise. You want to emulate, or more accurately, become a large bird, like a crane.

Beginning with the feet together . . . as if standing on a muddy shore . . . sunlight warming the body . . . and inhaling as the arms rise out and up like two large graceful wings opening and spreading to absorb the life-giving sunlight . . . hands meeting above the head and exhaling as the arms fold in front of the body with the palms facing the head as the body sinks slightly into the posture . . . not too deeply . . . just a slight sink . . . keeping the back straight . . . and then inhaling as the wings/arms open and rise out and up . . . and then folding in front . . . exhaling and sinking . . . repeating at your own pace . . . and have fun . . . try to be as birdlike as you can . . . try to feel what a bird feels . . . try to be a bird . . . at one . . . connected . . . in tune with everything . . . inhaling and exhaling as the body deems fit . . . not perfect . . . not precise . . . just graceful . . . just open . . . just receptive . . . however the movements feel best to you . . . and breathe.

(Pause) . . . (Pause)

And, when you are ready, return to stillness . . . arms resting at your sides . . . feet firmly rooted in the earth . . .

With an attitude of gratitude we begin the next posture . . . it is a posture of giving . . . of sharing. A way of giving back a little of our energy in appreciation for all that we have received. For all that has sustained us up to this point in our lives . . . in our recoveries . . . in our practices.

Beginning with the feet in a comfortable stance, about shoulder width apart . . . arms hanging loosely at your sides . . . tongue resting lightly on the roof of the mouth . . . inhaling and letting the arms rise up along the sides of the body with the hands facing the body, as if gathering chi from the body . . . still rising . . . when the hands rise up to a level about waist high the arms start to move out from the body with the hands facing upward . . . continuing in this universal gesture of giving . . . of offering, until they are above the head and lifted up . . . all on the inhale . . . and then the palms turn over and the arms float down to the sides as if on a cloud . . . and inhaling . . . hands gathering . . . arms pulling up along the sides . . . then reaching out toward heaven . . . toward the universe . . . toward the Great Mystery . . . toward whatever is Known . . . or Unknown . . . and exhaling . . . floating down . . . continuing in this way for a few repetitions . . . letting the breath and the heart lead the pace . . . in the silence . . . offering . . . sharing with the universe . . . out into infinity . . . out past, the concept of what we know . . . to the Tao . . . to the universal source . . . to that which cannot be named.

(Pause) . . . (Pause)

And, when you are ready, allowing the arms to remain by your sides . . . eyes closed . . . perhaps a slight smile on the face . . .

As this practice comes to an end we will move into a tonifying sequence. A sequence of exercises designed to stimulate the chi and allow it to smooth out and to go wherever it needs to go . . . again the emphasis will be on softness . . . on sensation . . . on the breath . . . on letting go of precision . . . of exactness . . . of perfection . . . have fun and smile!

With the feet positioned a little wider this time . . . allowing the hands to come together on the inhale . . . in front of the lower abdomen . . . gathering . . . and now exhaling as the arms rise in front of the body, outstretched . . . ascending . . . and now inhaling as the arms spread out to extend from opposite directions, shoulder height . . . expanding . . . and exhaling as the arms, still outstretched, move toward one another in front of the body, shoulder height, hands facing each other . . . contracting . . . now, inhaling, hands turn to face toward the body as they move in toward the face . . . pulling in . . . and hands turn facing outward . . . exhaling, as the arms extend back out in front of the body . . . pushing out . . . and now, inhaling as the arms float down, still extended . . . in sync with the exhale . . . descending . . . palms facing each other . . . and separating the hands and arms as the body exhales . . . dispersing.

(Pause)

And repeating . . . inhale . . . gathering . . . exhale . . . ascending . . . inhale . . . expanding . . . exhale . . . contracting . . .

Inhale . . . pulling in . . . exhale . . . pushing out . . . and inhale . . . descending . . . exhale . . . dispersing . . . and continuing as best as you can . . . allowing the breath . . . the breath that is present for you . . . to determine the pace and rhythm of the movements . . . perhaps rocking forward and backward slightly as the arms move in space . . . supported and guided by the dynamic force of the breath . . . by the force of chi . . . however that is for you . . . ascending . . . expanding . . . contracting . . . pulling in . . . pushing out . . . descending . . . dispersing . . . inhale . . . joining . . . exhale . . . rising . . . inhale . . . opening . . . exhale . . . closing . . . inhale . . . pulling . . . exhale . . . pushing . . . inhale . . . sinking . . . exhale . . . scattering . . . continuing on your own in silence for a couple of repetitions.

(Pause) . . . (Pause) . . . (Pause) . . . (Pause)

And coming to stillness when you are ready . . . arms resting by your sides . . . legs still a little wider than the shoulders . . . allowing the arms to curve around, the hands facing the body . . . hands facing the Tan Tien . . . curved and rounded as if supporting a big ball between the body and the hands and arms . . . sinking slightly into this stance . . . and feeling . . . the body . . . the ground . . . sensing the roots beneath the ground . . . extending out from the body through the feet . . . strong . . . secure . . . connected . . . stable . . . alive . . . and turning the hands out and open toward the earth as they scoop downward toward the earth . . . inhaling . . . as they rise . . . out and up . . . meeting above the head . . . and exhaling as they descend in front of the body . . . showering the body with chi . . . and again . . . inhaling and reaching into the earth, gathering and arms big and graceful . . . out and up in a big circle toward heaven . . . meeting and exhaling . . . descending in front of the body . . . and one last time . . . inhaling deep, deep extension with the arms into the earth, grabbing earth energy . . . arms rising out and up . . . mixing earth energy with energy from heaven and exhaling . . . arms and hands descending as chi showers and seals what has been cultivated deep inside the body.

(Pause)

And bowing . . .

"Bowing to that which got us here, and resting in that which we have become."[11]

In Closing

Pali is the language into which the Buddha's teachings were first transcribed thousands of years ago. **Samvega** is a word from the Pali language and one of my favorite descriptors in the Buddhist teachings. It is indicative of what many addicts experience upon entering recovery without having such a succinct word with which to name it. As translated by one contemporary Buddhist monk, Samvega is used to describe "the oppressive sense of shock, dismay, and alienation that comes with realizing the futility and meaninglessness of life as it's normally lived; a chastening sense of one's own complacency and foolishness in having let oneself live so blindly; and an anxious sense of urgency in trying to find a way out of the meaningless cycle."[12]

To me this word represents the beginning and the end, the alpha and the omega. It is an accurate description of what I felt when I first decided that drugs were an appropriate response to how I viewed life (the alpha), and then again when I stared out my kitchen window that fateful day and realized that this strategy had failed (the omega). It applies to both instances, one entirely destructive and the other life-saving. Both stem from a pervading sense of dissatisfaction.

I am happy to report that this state of mind no longer pervades my life. I have seen my Samvega progress into **Pasada**, which is another Pali word that means "clarity and serene confidence." I live my life most days with an attitude of contentment and serenity that is the direct result of seeing the true nature of my experience and my heartfelt acceptance of it. The steps, my higher power, chi, and mindfulness are now so inextricably entwined as to be inseparable in my life. This path of integrating Chi Kung and mindfulness into my recovery has been long and arduous. My hope is that this book will help ease your own exploration of the benefits of Chi Kung and mindfulness. May you find what I have found on this road to a truly balanced and centered recovery. Be patient, be diligent, and trust the process.

GLOSSARY

Acupuncture. Acupuncture originated in China centuries ago and is one of the main practices within Traditional Chinese Medicine (TCM). It consists of stimulating particular points in the body in specific ways in order to correct imbalances of energy flow in certain organs or the entire body itself. These imbalances consist of either too much chi (stagnation) or too little chi (depletion), and are believed to be the source of all ailments in the human body.

Acupuncture point. These are specific points along a meridian that can be pressed with fingers or stimulated with special needles to achieve very specific effects in the body. They usually have picturesque names, as well as designated letters and numbers that indicate which organ a given point corresponds to and where it is located on the meridian. For example: "Bubbling Well" (Yongquan) K1 refers to Kidney point number one on the bottom of the foot.

Ba Duan Jin. See Eight Section Brocade.

Bai Hui. Translated as "The hundred meeting place," this is an acupuncture point located on the very top of the head. Its numerical designation is GV20 or Governing Vessel 20. It is located approximately where the bones of the skull converge. It is considered an important point for both spirituality and health. It is where six of the major chi meridians connect with the governing and conception meridians—a place of great connectivity and receptivity.

Bodhidharma ("TaMo" in Chinese). The twenty-eighth Patriarch of Buddhism in a lineage that is traceable all the way back to Shakyamuni Buddha. He lived during the fifth and sixth centuries CE. Although he is the twenty-eigth Patriarch of Buddhism, he is considered the First Patriarch of Ch'an Buddhism in China. It is Bodhidharma who is credited with bringing Ch'an along with various "health exercises" to the Shaolin temples in China, thus beginning the intermingling of health, martial arts, and Ch'an Buddhism for which these Shaolin temples became famous. Bodhidharma, or "TaMo" in Chinese, is often referred to as "The Blue-eyed Barbarian" in Chinese texts.

Ch'an (Chinese for "Zen"). Even though Ch'an predated Zen Buddhism, it is Zen that most people are familiar with so it is often referred to as "Chinese Zen" for reference. Mahayana Buddhism is believed to have traveled to China from India along the Silk Road as a by-product of trade. Translations of Buddhist texts were made available during the prosperous Tang Dynasty period (618 to 907 CE). Aspects of Taoism were included so that a particularly Chinese version of Buddhism arose that became Ch'an, which is in fact a Chinese version of the Indian import. Bodhidharma is credited with the actual transmission of this "non-scripture" based variant of Buddhism that became very popular in the mountains and forests at the time. The word Ch'an is derived from the Sanskrit word *dyana*, which means "absorption" or "meditative state." This is actually the main emphasis of Ch'an Buddhism, which puts less value on the sutras (discourses of the Buddha) and instead focuses on meditation and direct experience as the main path to enlightenment. When Ch'an traveled to Japan it became "Zen," which is a derivative of the Middle Chinese word *dzyen*.

Chen Style Tai Chi Chuan. This is the original style of Tai Chi Chuan, originating in Chen Village, Henan Province, China. The agreed upon founder is Chen Wangting. This is the style of Tai Chi Chuan from which all others are derived. It was a closely guarded secret family style that was not taught outside of Chen Village until 1928. It is characterized by both fast and slow speeds with stomping and explosive techniques know as "fa jin." Although all Tai Chi Chuan styles are considered martial arts, Chen is the one most closely aligned with this fact.

Chi (Qi). Pronounced "chee," it can also be spelled "C'hi" to indicate Life force. Literally it translates as "breath." In the West it is known as bioelectrical energy when referring to chi in the body. However, chi is in all things. Chi is natural energy.

Dashi. Literally translated as "great master," it is the title of respect for masters of Chinese martial arts schools.

Dao Yin. Literally translated as "guiding and stretching," Dao Yin exercises are the precursor to Chi Kung and generally emphasized stretching of the tendons, muscles, and ligaments, often in coordination with the breath.

Digeridoo. A wind instrument invented and used by indigenous people in Australia. It is a hollow cylinder with a mouthpiece approximately three inches in diameter and a length that varies considerably. It is usually three to four feet long and produces a drone-like sound when air is manipulated into it from the player's mouth.

Eight Immortals. A legendary group of figures common in Chinese mythology and Taoism. They were human beings who attained immortality or deity-like status and powers by virtue of their lives on earth. They are believed to assist people with healings or by dispelling evil influences. They are regarded as heroes and deities by Taoists.

Eight Section Brocade ("Ba Duan Jin"). One of the most common "forms" of Chi Kung generally believed to be safe and effective for improving health. "Eight" refers to the number of individual postures in the form and "Brocade" refers to the integrated quality of one's energy and body that is believed to be the result of regular practice. Like the "silk brocade" very common in China in ancient times. Additionally, it provides a poetic way of remembering the exercises.

Etheric Body. An energetic field that surrounds the physical human body that is connected to that body or a part of it. The extent to which that "body" varies from individual to individual, and people's ability to sense or feel their etheric body varies. Sensitivity or "awareness" of this body can be cultivated through energy exercises like Chi Kung.

Five Element Theory. The theory upon which Traditional Chinese Medicine is based, developed by studying various processes, functions, and characteristics in nature. Five Element Theory maintains that all substances can be divided into one of five basic elements: earth, metal, water, wood, and fire. Each of these contains their own properties and characteristics. This theory can be applied to the functions and processes within the human body, where each organ is aligned with a specific element and in turn supports other organs according to the elemental properties and the natural inclination of each organ. For instance, the liver organ is associated with the wood element and is supportive of the heart, which is the fire element; wood nourishes fire. Imbalances in any of these areas (disease) are restored to harmony according to the interrelated properties of these elements.

Five Strains. These are normal human activities that, when performed for a prolonged period of time, are considered a "strain" on the body, particularly the yin organs. The five strains are extensive walking, standing, sitting, lying down, and prolonged use of the eyes.

Flexitarian. A vegetarian who occasionally eats meat, fish, or other types of animal protein.

Golden Dragon Temple. The Taoist temple located in Southern China that Master Share Lew was a direct lineage descendent of. Master Share Lew fled China during the Cultural Revolution and eventually founded the Taoist Sanctuary in San Diego, CA.

Golden Elixir Style of Internal Alchemy. The particular method of internal cultivation of chi that emphasized spiritual immortality. It is said to have first been developed by Lu Dongbin and Chong Li, two of the Eight Immortals.

Hui Yin. Translated as "meeting of yin," it is an acupuncture point located at the bottom of the torso, in between the anus and the reproductive organs, at the center of the perineum. Its numerical designation is CV1 or Conception Vessel 1. It is another very powerful point and is frequently used and referenced in Chi Kung. Often a connection between the Hui Yin and the Bai Hui (top of head) is visualized in Chi Kung.

Immortality. When Taoists refer to immortality they don't mean the immortality of the "physical body" but the immortality of the "spiritual body," where our spirit or our essence resides after our physical bodies have failed us. The spiritual self is cultivated to a degree so that it can live on forever. In this way Taoists believe you can transcend the limits of the physical body and go where the physical cannot, like the fourth dimension or the spirit world. The Chinese word for this is *xian*, a spiritual/celestial being or an enlightened being.

Internal Alchemy (Neidan). The Taoist practice of gathering, storing, and circulating energy or chi within the body. In this sense it can be synonymous with Chi Kung.

Internal Martial Arts. Traditional Chinese martial arts styles that emphasize internal (chi) cultivation as an adjunct to physical power in their applications. Tai Chi Chuan, Bagua Chang and Hsing Yi Chuan are the most popular styles.

Interoception. The sense of knowing how your body is feeling from the inside. This is a felt-sense of the body that can be refined with meditative methods like the Body Scan.

Kung Fu (Gongfu, Gungfu). Pronounced "gung foo," the term is generally accepted in the West to refer to Chinese martial arts. However, the words actually mean "skill achieved through hard work or patience" and can refer to any type of skill, not just martial arts. Thus, one could achieve Kung Fu in writing, cooking, or any variety of tasks in which skill is accrued. It was only in the late twentieth century that it became synonymous with Chinese martial arts.

Lao Gong. Translated as "palace of toil," it is an acupuncture point located in the center of each palm. Its numerical designation is P8 or Pericardium 8, and it is the eighth point on the pericardium meridian. In Chi Kung it is known to be a point where chi can be easily emitted from the body. Hence it is invaluable to reiki practitioners and most energetic healers. It is also referenced as being extremely powerful in martial arts applications, particularly the internal styles (see Internal Martial Arts). It is also possible to absorb chi through this point, which we experience in the Single Arm posture of the Eight Section Brocade.

Long Fist Style of Kung Fu (Chanquan). A style of martial arts in China in which fully extended kicks and striking techniques are used. It is famous for its leaping, jumping, and sweeping leg movements combined with long extended arm movements that are intended to devastate opponents. It has a close association with the Shaolin temple and is considered a long range fighting style that can cover a lot of ground in the scope of its attack. It has many acrobatic aspects and it takes a great deal of skill to perfect the execution of its moves.

Lu Dongbin. A historical figure who is believed to have attained immortality and one of the Eight Immortals spoken of in Taoist mythology. Lu Dongbin is often represented as a scholarly figure who carries a sword on his back to dispel evil spirits. He is considered one of the masters of Internal Alchemy practiced in Taoism. He is portrayed as clever and eager to help people gain wisdom or learn the Tao. The Eight Immortals also are imbued with human behavioral flaws. Lu is said to be a ladies' man and prone to bouts of drunkenness, which is not uncommon among the Eight Immortals. Most likely people took comfort in these deities who were fun loving yet capable of powerful spiritual assistance if invoked.

Ma Bu (horse stance). This is a standard stance in Chinese martial arts. In Kung Fu it is typically wide with the thighs parallel to the ground and the back straight. In Tai Chi the legs are wide and the back is straight but the stance is not as deep, the inner thighs and seat are rounded as if sitting on a horse.

Mahayana. Translated as "great vehicle," this tradition developed and spread from India and is a much later version of Buddhism. It is still practiced today and is the most popular form of Buddhism in the world. Although there are always similarities between the different schools there are certain distinctions as well. Mahayana's principle difference is the focus on the *bodhisattva ideal* or the aspiration to forgo complete enlightenment until all beings are free from suffering. Thus it is believed to be a tradition that emphasizes compassion for others as a primary motivating factor.

Meridian. A pathway through which chi travels in the body. There are twelve major meridians in the body and numerous branches that correspond to all the organs and systems in the body. These meridians are used in acupuncture, acupressure massage, and Chi Kung.

Mindfulness. Paying attention in a deliberate way in the present moment without judgment. It is attentive awareness of the "way things really are," and it is considered one of the seven factors of Enlightenment in Buddhism—Enlightenment being freedom from suffering or complete release from greed, hatred, and delusion. Although mindfulness is inextricably linked to Buddhism and specific meditation practices within that tradition, it is gaining popularity as a secular practice in Western psychology and various modern modalities like Mindfulness-Based Stress Reduction and Mindfulness-Based Relapse Prevention.

Ming Men. Translated as "life's door" or "gate of life." It is an acupuncture point located directly behind the belly button on the spine. Its numerical designation is GV4 or Governing Vessel 4. This point is used extensively in Chi Kung work.

Oxygen Therapy. Oxygen therapy is a treatment that provides a patient with extra oxygen, that is, oxygen in addition to what is readily available through normal breathing of available air. It is helpful for conditions or diseases that limit, obstruct, or interfere with normal healthy respiration. It has also been used to increase levels of oxygen within specific cells or tissue of the body. Insufficient cellular oxygen levels create a condition called hypoxia, which has been linked to pain in chronic pain sufferers.

Pali. The ancient Indo-Aryan language into which the teachings and discourses of the Buddha were first translated. Although not commonly believed to be the actual language the Buddha spoke, it is still regarded as very close to his dialect. Consequently, these early written representations of the Buddha's words are called the Pali Canon and they are quite extensive. Generally when Pali words are used, the reference is to the Theravadan tradition of Buddhism and when Sanskrit words are used the reference is to the Mahayana tradition.

Pasada. A Pali word meaning "clarity and serene confidence." It is usually found in conjunction with Samvega in the Buddhist texts and is seen as an appropriate development in the state of mind as practitioners progress from the disillusionment that inspires change to an understanding of the way things are and confidence in one's ability to walk a path toward liberation.

Pranayama. A Sanskrit term that translates as "extension of life-force or breath." It is usually encountered as an auxiliary practice of Yoga. Prana is the Indian equivalent of the Chinese term chi (qi).

Proprioception. The sense of knowing and feeling one's own body and its parts relative to each other whether still or moving in space. It is what allows us to eat with a fork without having to stop and calculate distance and movement in order to place food in our mouth. It is also what allows us to use our arms and hands and feet to drive a car while looking at the roadway.

Qi. See Chi.

Quanzhen School (Complete reality school). Originating in Northern China in the twelfth century, it was a school of Taoism, which used internal alchemy as a road to immortality. It was dedicated to the use of methods inside the body (neidan) as opposed to (waidan), which used external things like herbs, minerals, and various concoctions that proved both dangerous and deadly. The Quanzhen school is concerned with longevity and immortality and uses the Yin-Yang theory and the Five Element Theory to harmonize with the Tao.

Reiki. A Japanese spiritual healing technique in which life force energy or ki (chi in Chinese) is manipulated or facilitated by the practitioner to impart an effect on the client by laying hands either on or near the surface of the body.

Samvega. A Pali word that refers to the oppressive sense of shock or dismay that comes from realizing the meaninglessness of life as it is normally lived. Also included is a sense of foolishness for having lived this way, culminating in a sense of urgency to find a way out of this meaninglessness cycle.

Sanskrit. An Indo-Aryan language common to Hinduism, Jainism, and Buddhism. Much of the Mahayana scriptures were translated into Sanskrit.

Seven Impairments. Normal human activities that impair the optimal function of the body and mind. They are: overeating, fury, cold weather, sorrow, anxiety, laziness (lack of energy), and extreme temperature changes.

Shaolin Kung Fu. Originally the martial art system that grew out of the combination of Ch'an Buddhism and martial arts in the sixth century at the Shaolin monastery in Henan province, China.

Shaolin Temple. The word "Shaolin" roughly translates as "forest monastery." Specifically, it refers to the Ch'an Buddhist temple on Mount Song in Henan province in China. This temple is famous for its association with Chinese martial arts and the development of Shaolin Kung Fu. Bodhidharma became the first abbot of this monastery and the inspiration for incorporating exercise and martial arts into the regime of the monks who spent long hours meditating.

Sifu (Shifu). "Teacher-father" title of respect in Chinese martial arts schools.

Sponsor. Within the context of twelve-step fellowships, this is a person who helps guide one through the Twelve Steps and shows that person how to apply the steps in his or her life.

Tai Chi (Taiji). Shortened version of Tai Chi Chuan, could possibly indicate that the martial art aspect is unknown or deemphasized by practitioner, teacher, or both.

Tai Chi Chuan (Taijiquan). "Supreme Ultimate Fist"—a martial art that utilizes chi and soft flowing movements as a means for self-defense and health. It is referred to as an *internal* martial art, indicating that the strength or power used comes from inside the body, or the chi, as opposed to brute muscular strength.

Tan Tien. Translated as "elixir field," there are three Tan Tiens in the body but this book only focuses on the "lower" Tan Tien, located approximately three inches below the navel and three inches inside the abdomen. This lower Tan Tien is the collection point for energy or chi in the body. It is sometimes called the "Ocean or Sea of chi" for this reason.

Tantra. The style of rituals, meditations, and practices that seek to unify the human spirit with the divine. In the West it is most readily recognized as the practice of "spiritual sex" or "divine sexuality." In truth the sexual practices found in tantra comprise only a small part of this elaborate system of purification and realization.

Tao (Dao). Translated as "Way or Path" and pronounced "dow," it is the basic guiding or defining principle of Taoism. The Tao is the source and the force that drives all creation. It is the equivalent of the "spirit that moves in all things" that is a cornerstone of Native American spirituality. The Tao is balance, harmony, and flow.

Taoism. Pronounced "dowism," it is the philosophy or practice of being in harmony with life. Taoism is considered one of the three major religions (philosophies) in China. The other two are Confucianism and Buddhism. Very often they are blended together. The degree to which they are blended depends on which sect or school of Taoism is being represented. All the schools have a very strong emphasis on harmony and balance. Many incorporate physical exercises to help with this harmonious integration. Chi Kung and Tai Chi Chuan are practices that figure prominently in Taoism. The Yin-Yang symbol is representative of Taoism and Tai Chi. It is usually depicted as a circle with a reverse S- shape down the middle delineating a black and a white tear drop shaped portion. In the white portion there is a black dot (the eye) and in the black portion there is a white dot (the eye). The Quanzhen School of Taoism was founded in Shandong province in the twelfth century. It became the largest and most influential school in China throughout the thirteenth and fourteenth centuries.

Tien Gunn (Celestial stem). Sometimes also referred to as the "taiji pole," it is an imaginary column of energy that runs from heaven through the Bai Hui on the top of the head through the Hui Yin at the perineum and deep into the center of the earth.

Traditional Chinese Medicine (TCM). A practice of medicine in China that goes back thousands of years and utilizes but is not limited to herbal preparations, acupuncture, acupressure, and Chi Kung to affect healing of various ailments. It is considered an alternative medical practice. TCM incorporates principles of Yin-Yang theory, Five Elements Theory, and chi in its usage.

Treasure Vase Breathing Exercises (Bao Ping Qi). Originating in Tibet as part of the Tantrayana practice, it is a type of breathing very similar to Tan Tien breathing except more force is used at certain points and the breath is held at other points. A qualified teacher should be sought for this type of practice because misuse or incorrect practice could be harmful, which is why no details are given here. Many of the tantra practices have a strong shamanic influence in them.

Triple Warmer (San Jiao). The Triple Warmer is located in the torso and has three parts: The upper warmer located in the heart and lung region, the middle warmer located in the stomach region, and the lower warmer in the pelvic girdle where the reproductive and eliminating organs are. The only physical organ associated with the Triple Warmer is the hypothalamus, which is recognized as the "thermostat" for the body, and is located in the cranial cavity. The Triple Warmer is not a physical organ, it is more like a regulatory system. The Triple Warmer governs the endocrine system, the autonomic nervous system, basic drives, and appetite. The job of the Triple Warmer is to coordinate all the bodily functions in the trunk.

Vajrayana. Translated as "diamond way," this is a style of Buddhism common in Tibet that focuses on tantric practices, which are designed to unify heaven and earth within the human form. Various techniques involving chanting, visualization, and mudras are used to achieve results up to and including enlightenment or magical powers. There is also a pantheon of deities and celestial beings that are incorporated into many of these meditations and practices.

Vipassana. A Pali word that translates as "seeing clearly" or "seeing things as they really are." It is a meditation style with roots in Theravadan Buddhism with emphasis on awareness and being present to one's experience. It is the inspiration for the various mindfulness practices that have become so useful and popular in our present day society.

Wu Chi. Pronounced "woo chee," it means Nothing, Empty, Boundless, or Limitless.

Wu Style Tai Chi Chuan. "Wu" is a family name that refers to one of the four main styles of Tai Chi Chuan. It was founded by Wu Ch'uan-yu. This style was developed after Yang and Chen and is characterized by a leaning type of stance that is deceptively stable and well suited to martial applications.

Yang Style Tai Chi Chuan. A style of Tai Chi Chuan developed by Yang Lu-ch'an as a derivative of Chen Style Tai Chi Chuan. Yang style is one of the four main styles practiced today. It is the most widely known and practiced style in the world and the one most people have seen performed. It is characterized by slow flowing movements and an upright posture which is kept relatively even throughout most of the form.

Yin organs. In Traditional Chinese Medicine, the yin organs are the heart, liver, spleen, kidneys, and lungs. The function of the yin organs is to produce or transform vital substances like blood, chi (considered fluid by its nature), and any other bodily fluids. The organ's relationship to other organs is more important in TCM than its basic anatomical structure. There are also yang organs: the stomach, the bladder, the gall bladder, the small intestines, and the large intestines. Sometimes there are considered to be six yin organs with the pericardium added and six yang organs with the Triple Warmer added, for which there is no distinct physical structure. Just as the Yin-Yang symbol itself represents harmony, TCM is based on enhancing a harmonious relationship between all the functional units of the body, especially the paired connections between the yin-yang organs.

Yin-Yang. A concept in Taoist philosophy in which contrary or seemingly opposite forces or things are in fact interconnected. Examples of such opposites or contrary pairs are female and male, light and dark, hot and cold, life and death, soft and hard, and open and closed. So when used in reference to a movement like yin-yang ribs, it imparts that quality of opening and closing, soft and hard in the actual rotation of the waist and upper body.

Yogic. Of or pertaining to the practice of yoga, which literally translates as "union" or "joining." Yoga is recognized in the West as a series of particular poses or postures that are performed in an effort to stretch, energize, strengthen, and harmonize the body. Many believe that yoga was developed as a practice to condition the body to be better able to sustain static meditation postures. There are numerous styles and disciplines of yoga, each with a little different emphasis on some part of the practice.

Zen. A school of Mahayana Buddhism that grew out of Ch'an Buddhism from China.

NOTES

1 John Stuart Reid and Annaliese Kohinoor, "Rediscovering the Art and Science of Sound Healing," *Caduceus Magazine* 72 (September 2010): 18–21.

2 James McMurtry, "Ruby and Carlos," lyrics, *Just Us Kids*, Lightning Rod Records, 2008. © James McMurtry.

3 Narcotics Anonymous, *Narcotics Anonymous* (Van Nuys, CA: NA World Services, Inc, 1983), 87. Reprinted by permission of NA World Services, Inc. All rights reserved.

4 Narcotics Anonymous, *Narcotics Anonymous* (Van Nuys, CA: NA World Services, Inc, 1983), 18. Reprinted by permission of NA World Services, Inc. All rights reserved.

5 Mel Pohl, MD, FASAM, *A Day Without Pain* (Las Vegas: Central Recovery Press, 2008), 135.

6 Kevin Griffin, *A Burning Desire* (Carlsbad, CA: Hay House, 2010), 29. Used with permission.

7 Ibid.

8 Stephen Batchelor, "Foundations of Mindfulness," *Tricycle Magazine*, July 2012, http://www.tricycle.com/new-buddhism/mental-discipline/foundations-mindfulness.

9 Stephen Batchelor, *Foundations of Mindfulness* (Tricycle Magazine, 2010), PDF e-book, 3.

10 See the video "Widening the Circle" on the Center for Mindfulness website at http://www.mindful.org/video/widening-the-circle-of-mindfulness.

11 Heather Sundberg's practice.

12 Thānissaro Bhikkhu, "Affirming the Truths of the Heart: The Buddhist Teachings on Samvega & Pasada," *Access to Insight*, 8 March 2011, http://www.accesstoinsight.org/lib/authors/thanissaro/affirming.html.